BIBLE QUIZZES & GAMES

CRYSTAL BOWMAN & TERI McKINLEY

Discovery House.
from Our Daily Bread Ministries

Printed in the United States of America
Second printing in 2019

OUR DAILY BREAD FOR KIDS

OUR DAILY BREAD FOR KIDS
BIBLE QUIZZES & GAMES

Hey, there! How exciting that you have this book! You're going to learn some important things about the Bible while having lots of fun!

These pages are filled with quizzes and puzzles that focus on stories and characters from the beginning of the Bible to the end. Some of the puzzles may challenge your brain power, so use the Bible verse hints if you need help. Each quiz is followed by a related picture puzzle, a word search, and a crossword. All the answers are found in the back of the book.

Are you ready? Let's go! Have fun as you learn more about the most important Book of all.

KNOW YOUR BIBLE

Many different people wrote down the books of the Bible, but God is the real author. His Holy Spirit guided all the Bible writers. God used people to write the words, but He told each one what to say.

WHAT DO YOU KNOW ABOUT THE BIBLE?

1. **Who wrote the first 5 books of the Bible? (Deuteronomy 31:24)**
   - **a)** Adam
   - **b)** Abraham
   - **c)** Moses
   - **d)** Jacob

2. Who wrote many of the other Old Testament books? (Hebrews 1:1)

    a) prophets
    b) shepherds
    c) judges
    d) doctors

3. How many books are in the Old Testament? (See table of contents in your Bible)

    a) 24
    b) 39
    c) 35
    d) 47

4. Why were many of the Psalms written? (Psalm 95:1-2)

    a) to teach kids how to read
    b) to learn about shepherds
    c) for praising God and singing
    d) for bedtime stories

5. What exciting story is found in Luke chapter 2?

    a) the crossing of the Red Sea
    b) the birth of Jesus
    c) Daniel in the lions' den
    d) David and Goliath

6. **Why was the book of John written?**
   (John 20:31)
   a) the author liked to tell stories
   b) the author wanted to be famous
   c) to show people what good writing is
   d) so people would believe in Jesus

7. **How many books are in the New Testament?**
   (See table of contents in your Bible)
   a) 12
   b) 20
   c) 27
   d) 66

8. **Who wrote many of the books in the New Testament? (Romans 1:1)**
   a) Jonah
   b) Lazarus
   c) Zacchaeus
   d) the apostle Paul

Find the answers on page 133

SPOT THE DIFFERENCE

Draw a line between the matching pairs of Bibles.

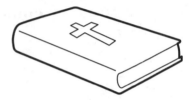

Find the answers on page 133

CROSSWORD PUZZLE

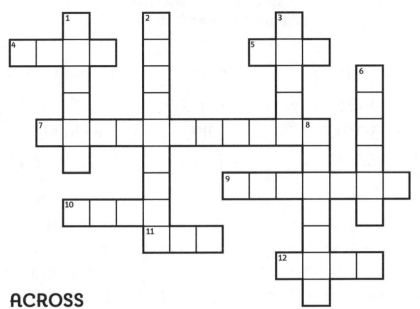

ACROSS

4. All the words in the Bible are _____ (Psalm 119:160)
5. The real author of the Bible (2 Timothy 3:16)
7. What we receive when we tell God we are sorry for our sins (Acts 2:38)
9. Who wrote many of the Proverbs? (Proverbs 1:1)
10. The Bible helps us learn about God's _____ (John 3:16)
11. When you disobey it is called _____ (1 John 5:17)
12. The more you _____ the Bible, the more you will learn about God

DOWN

1. A person who writes a book
2. Jesus's followers (Matthew 10:1)
3. There are sixty-six _____ in the Bible
6. Jesus came to be our _____ (Philippians 3:20)
8. The Bible has lots of good _____

Find the answers on page 134

WORD SEARCH
Can you find all the words?
Words may be forward, up-and-down, or diagonal.

AUTHOR	GOD	PAUL
BIBLE	JESUS	PROPHETS
BOOKS	LUKE	PSALMS
DISCIPLES	MOSES	TESTAMENT

```
W Y M T C R D I S C I P L E S M W V H Q
X M W M P D R T I K P T N L U K E C Y P
Y Q M D O M T X I R L T I M O R F Q R J
B C W M P S X B T V T L I N V C R W S E
I W X Q Z B E L P C V V T S B R Y P M S
B F K B W Q D S Q D S Z R U Q O L L I U
L K X M B D B P P K C G V G O D L T T S
E F R H D M N T T J B B D M L O Q X L R
L K T M B A U T H O R K L N M P B D R H
K T B Q N J W M H R B S N B Q M B X S F
W T E S T A M E N T W L T N P X K H C P
M P R O P H E T S M M N X T L T P N D A
Q T K N W S T Q P S A L M S D C H F Q U
K X V F M G D B K L R T S M B O O K S L
```

Find the answers on page 134

Quiz 2
GOD THE FATHER

God made everyone. And He gives us everything we need to live, just like good parents do for their kids. But He wants to do more than that— He wants to make us members of His own special family! Then we can call God "Father" because we are His own children.

**WHAT DO YOU KNOW ABOUT
GOD THE FATHER AND HIS CHILDREN?**

1. **Psalm 139:14 says the way God makes people is:**
   a) amazing and wonderful
   b) kind and unique
   c) fast and messy
   d) easy and great

2. **What is God's family called?**
   (1 Corinthians 12:27)
   a) the king's court
   b) the perfect family
   c) the body of Christ
   d) the disciples of Jesus

3. **John 3:16 says God loved the world so much that He:**
   a) made Sunday a day of rest
   b) sent manna from heaven
   c) created sunsets for us to enjoy
   d) gave His only Son to people

4. **How will other people know you are a child of God? (John 13:35)**
   a) if you read your Bible a lot
   b) if you love others
   c) if you go to church every week
   d) if you pray before you go to sleep

5. **How often does God go to sleep? (Psalm 121:1–4)**
   a) once a year
   b) two times a month
   c) once a week
   d) never

6. **Where should God's name be praised? (Psalm 113:3)**
   a) from where the sun rises to where it sets
   b) in the northern hemisphere
   c) in six continents
   d) on top of mountains

7. **What does the Bible say is God's masterpiece? (See Ephesians 2:10 NLT)**
   a) the Grand Canyon
   b) the Pacific Ocean
   c) people
   d) animals

8. **What can separate us from God's love? (Romans 8:38–39)**
   a) telling a lie
   b) nothing
   c) the future
   d) going far away

Find the answers on page 135

Find these words in the box below,* and cross out the letters as you go. We've done the first one for you as an example.

BIRD   CLOUD   GOOD   LORD   THANK
CARE   FISH   JESUS   MOTHER
CHILD   GIRL   KIND   SPIRIT

* The letters of each word are connected in a row, but they may read in ANY direction!

```
Y  O  U  G  R  S  M  H  H  E
A  V  I  E  P  N  O  L  S  Y
T  R  K  I  N  D  T  F  I  A
L  H  R  T  D  S  H  C  F  H
E  I  A  U  R  U  E  H  A  L
T  R  O  N  D  S  R  I  D  E
A  L  D  R  K  E  Y  L  O  L
C  K  I  N  O  J  W  D  O  S
A  B  E  R  A  C  L  R  G  L
Y  O  U  R  N  E  D  E  D  S
```

STEP TWO Copy the remaining letters to the spaces below to see the hidden message!

— — — —   — — — — — — — —   — — — — —

— — — — — — —   — — — — —   — — —

— — — —   — — — — — — .   (Matthew 6:32 NLT)

Find the answers on page 135

WORD SEARCH
Can you find all the words?
Words may be forward or backward.

AMAZING   FAMILY   SON
BODY OF CHRIST   FATHER   SUNSET
CHILDREN OF GOD   LOVE   WONDERFUL
CREATOR   MASTERPIECE   WORLD

```
          G H N                    S O N
        B E V O L                L M G S Q
      D V B Y H R S            M F A M I L Y
    V D B S U N S E T      Y P L K J H N O E
  S C D X Z D F R T H A M A Z I N G B D S
C R E A T O R K P K L M F B Y S Q C B N L V
B B O D Y O F C H R I S T N H N B M T H H B
X D S Z W R T H Y M A S T E R P I E C E X N
D N C H I L D R E N O F G O D N H B P D M N
  N H B P D C E L H N M B F A H T R V C N
    R F S D W P L K J H G D S N K Q D B
      D R T W O N D E R F U L H P L K
        H Y H G B N R W D B N M T H
          H G B R E H T A F M D S
            N D R F E E H T B V
              B W O R L D T H
                C B N R T D
                  R D W S
                    C D
```

Find the answers on page 135

CROSSWORD PUZZLE

ACROSS

5. Which book of the Bible says God made you "amazing and wonderful"? (139:14 NIrV)
6. When parents welcome a child who is not related to them into their family, it's called _____ (Romans 8:15)
7. God _____ His son, Jesus, to save us from sin (1 John 4:10)
8. When we believe in Jesus to forgive our sins, we become a part of God's _____ (Galatians 6:10)
9. What is another word for a king's child? (Romans 8:16–17 NLT)

DOWN

1. Who is a witness that we are heirs with Jesus? (see Romans 8:16–17)
2. Who must we believe in to become a part of God's family? (Acts 16:31)
3. Who can be a part of God's family? (John 7:37)
4. Who loves you forever? (Psalm 136:26)
5. What is the most important part of God's creation? (see Genesis 1:26)
6. What is another word for "father" in Romans 8:15?

Find the answers on page 136

Quiz 3
A SPECIAL CREATION

In the beginning, there was nothing but water and darkness. The earth was empty. It had no shape. But God was there before everything else, and He had a plan to create a world.

WHAT DO YOU KNOW ABOUT THE STORY OF CREATION?

1. **According to Genesis 1:1, when did God create "the heavens and the earth"?**
   a) billions of years ago
   b) 4000 BC
   c) in the beginning
   d) when the time was right

2. **What does the Bible say the brand-new earth was like? (Genesis 1:2)**
   a) bright and cheerful
   b) formless and empty
   c) sticky and gooey
   d) loud and busy

3. **How many days did God use to fill and complete His heavens and earth? (Genesis 1:31)**
   a) one
   b) two
   c) six
   d) twenty-one

4. **What did God think of His work after each day of creation? (Genesis 1:4, 10, 12, 18, 21, 25, 31)**
   a) it was cool
   b) it was right
   c) it was amazing
   d) it was good

5. **What was the first thing God put on the earth's dry ground? (Genesis 1:11–12)**
   a) human beings
   b) plants and trees
   c) animals and birds
   d) swings and teeter-totters

6. How does the Bible say God brought most of creation into being? (Genesis 1:3, 6, 9, 11, 14, 20, 24)
   a) He spoke
   b) He thought really hard
   c) He snapped His finger
   d) He waved His hand

7. The first human was made differently. What did God use to create Adam? (Genesis 2:7)
   a) animal bones
   b) tree sap
   c) clouds and rain
   d) dust of the earth

8. What place did God make as a home for Adam and his wife, Eve? (Genesis 2:15)
   a) the Mount of Olives
   b) the Pool of Siloam
   c) the Garden of Eden
   d) the Valley of Elah

Find the answers on page 136

Start

Help Adam and Eve find their way through the Garden.

End

Find the answer on page 136

CROSSWORD PUZZLE

ACROSS

3. Another name for our world (Genesis 1:1)
4. What name did God give to the darkness? (Genesis 1:5)
5. The name of the first woman (Genesis 3:20)
7. God made fish to live in the _____ (Genesis 1:21)
8. Besides human beings, what did God make on the sixth day? (Genesis 1:25)
10. To make something out of nothing (Genesis 1:1)
11. Who made everything? (Genesis 1:1)

DOWN

1. Another name for sky (Genesis 1:1)
2. In what book of the Bible can you read the story of creation?
6. The name of the garden God created (Genesis 2:8)
8. What name did God give to the first man? (Genesis 2:20)
9. What did God create on the first day? (Genesis 1:3)

Find the answers on page 137

WORD SEARCH
Can you find all the words?
Words may be forward or up-and-down.

ANIMALS	LIGHT	STARS
BIRDS	MOON	SUN
GARDEN	PEOPLE	TREES
GOOD	PLANTS	WATER

```
      E C P K L S R B P N
      S Q P E O P L E M N X Z
    G O O D P M S S T A R S D L
    R T Q C T M Q B C S N S M T T H
  Y T W F T G A R D E N P X M R R T M
  T P L C X A N I M A L S X W E Q V T
  K N L G T D M O O N T R L T E X Z R
  W A T E R Q H G N M P L K W S F X C
  T C X L M P L A N T S T B B W T R Y
    R T L I G H T S D C T I I Z X S
    T N Q V X Z S Q D T R R K D
      F G B H H U T Y L P D C
      O B N H N Z H B D S
```

Find the answers on page 137

Quiz 4
ADAM AND EVE AND SIN

Adam and Eve lived in the Garden of Eden. God told them they could eat the fruit from any tree in the garden except one. When they were tempted to disobey God, they gave in to that temptation. They sinned against God and brought much trouble into the world.

WHAT DO YOU KNOW ABOUT THE STORY OF ADAM AND EVE'S FIRST SIN?

1. Which animal tricked Eve into eating the fruit she wasn't supposed to eat? (Genesis 3:1)
   a) a monkey
   b) a sheep
   c) a snake
   d) a bird

2. **Who was with Eve when she sinned? (see Genesis 3:6)**
   a) Adam
   b) no one
   c) all of the animals
   d) her sister

3. **What was the snake's punishment for tricking Eve? (Genesis 3:14)**
   a) he had to leave the garden
   b) he had to crawl on his belly
   c) he had to eat plants
   d) he would be chased by other animals

4. **Who gave Adam the fruit to eat? (see Genesis 3:6)**
   a) the snake
   b) a monkey
   c) he picked it himself
   d) Eve

5. **How many trees were Adam and Eve allowed to eat from? (Genesis 3:1–3)**
   a) none
   b) all but one
   c) 10
   d) 50

6. **What was Adam's punishment for disobeying God? (Genesis 3:17–19)**
   a) he had to make clothes for himself and Eve
   b) he couldn't eat fruit any more
   c) he had to work hard for food
   d) he had to kill the snake

7. **What was Eve's punishment for disobeying God? (Genesis 3:16)**
   a) she had great pain when she gave birth to her children
   b) she had to help Adam work for food
   c) she was only allowed to eat meat
   d) she couldn't talk to Adam any more

8. **What did God do for Adam and Eve before they left the garden? (Genesis 3:21)**
   a) He gave them tools to hunt with
   b) He fed them
   c) He helped them build a house
   d) He made clothes for them

Find the answers on page 138

CROSSWORD PUZZLE

ACROSS

2. When we want to do something we know is wrong, it's called _____ (1 Corinthians 10:13)
5. The "forbidden fruit" Adam and Eve ate grew on a _____ (Genesis 2:17)
6. Adam's punishment was that he had to _____ hard for food (Genesis 3:23)
7. Eve's punishment was that she would have pain when she had _____ (Genesis 3:16)
10. There was only ____ tree Adam and Eve were not allowed to eat from (see Genesis 2:16–17)
11. God made clothes for Adam and Eve from animal _____ (Genesis 3:21)

DOWN

1. Who took the second bite of the fruit? (Genesis 3:6)
3. Who took the first bite of the fruit? (Genesis 3:6)
4. When Adam and Eve sinned, they realized they were _____ (Genesis 3:7)
8. When God came looking for Adam and Eve, they were _____ (see Genesis 3:10)
9. The name of the garden where Adam and Eve lived (Genesis 2:15)
11. The animal who tricked Eve (Genesis 3:1)

Find the answers on page 138

COLOR BY NUMBER
Can you find the hidden picture?
1=Brown   2=Green   3=Blue   4=Yellow   5=Purple   6=Red

WORD SEARCH
Can you find all the words?
Words may be forward or backward, up-and-down, or diagonal.

ADAM	EVE	HIDE
BITE	FORGIVENESS	SNAKE
CLOTHES	FRUIT	TEMPTATION
DISOBEY	GARDEN	TREE

```
G A D M A S D F K L P O C L O T H E S
A N O I H W A B N I W E B T S E M O I
R F S S E N E V I G R O F L A B S T K
D A N L N S W E L T L Y J E T D H O T
E L A E H L T I N S E L E O W I A H U
N M K Y I D R Y E A L O D M H S U M H
L T E M P T A T I O N M A S T O E D S
E M N I E K M R L V G C U N M B T H A
S O W L H I D E U F I T N E V E D E R
I T H M U A S E B R C K A W I Y B A O
A O S N C E I H A F R U I T V E H O N
```

Find the answers on page 138

OLD TESTAMENT HEROES
PART ONE

The Bible is filled with many exciting stories about people who loved God. Sometimes they had to do things that were hard. But because they loved God, they did what He wanted them to do.

LET'S SEE HOW WELL YOU KNOW THE STORIES OF NOAH, ABRAHAM, AND JOSEPH.

1. **According to Genesis 6:14, what did God tell Noah to do?**
   a) build a raft
   b) build a bridge
   c) build an ark
   d) take swimming lessons

2. Why did God want to send a flood to cover the earth? (Genesis 6:5)
   a) the people were very sinful
   b) the trees needed water
   c) the fish needed more room to swim
   d) Noah had prayed for rain

3. How long did it rain after Noah and his family went inside the ark? (Genesis 7:12)
   a) two years
   b) four months
   c) twenty-five weeks
   d) forty days and forty nights

4. According to Genesis 12:1, what did God tell Abram to do?
   a) go on vacation
   b) get a job
   c) get married
   d) leave his country and his family

5. What promise did God make to Abram? (see Genesis 12:2)
   a) his wife would have twins
   b) he would be a king
   c) his family would become a great nation
   d) he would live for 300 years

6. **What new name did God give to Abram? (Genesis 17:5)**
   a) Abe
   b) Abraham
   c) Isaac
   d) Israel

7. **What did Joseph's brothers do to him? (Genesis 37:28)**
   a) they made a pretty coat for him
   b) they gave him a crown to wear
   c) they sold him as a slave
   d) they hid him in a cave

8. **How did God use Joseph? (Genesis 41:41)**
   a) Joseph built a big city
   b) Joseph became an important ruler in Egypt
   c) Joseph fought wild animals
   d) Joseph taught people how to make bricks

Find the answers on page 139

DECORATE JOSEPH'S COAT

What do you think Joseph's colorful coat looked like?

CROSSWORD PUZZLE

ACROSS

4. The name of Abraham's son (Genesis 21:3)
5. God told Abraham he would have many _____ (Genesis 16:10)
8. Joseph _____ his brothers for being mean to him (see Genesis 50:18–21)
10. The name of Abraham's wife (Genesis 17:15)
11. The opposite of wrong
12. Noah brought his _____ into the ark with him (Genesis 7:1)

DOWN

1. What sign did God place in the sky after the flood? (Genesis 9:13)
2. God sent rain for forty _____ and nights (Genesis 7:4)
3. How many brothers did Joseph have? (see Genesis 37:9)
6. God told Abraham to leave his _____(Genesis 12:1)
7. Who built the ark? (Genesis 7:1)
9. To do what God wants us to do

Find the answers on page 139

WORD SEARCH
Can you find all the words?
Words may be forward, backward, or up-and-down.

ABRAHAM	GENESIS	PROMISE
ARK	JOSEPH	RAIN
EGYPT	NATION	RULER
FLOOD	NOAH	SLAVE

```
H G T L S L A V E D V B C W A X S B M Q F
L D G B V C X Z W N A T I O N M B W Q G L
C H R R E B N M K P C Q W R T Y P M K G O
N B U V D N A T P C N M H B K L P K W B O
O X L D W Q S T M T P Y G E D W S Z Q R D
A F E T H W M Q B A R K T H G D S W Q S T
H G R B B Q V W N R Q G H G E N E S I S M
Y R T H G D C B M J O S E P H W G H M Q L
S G H K L A B R A H A M M R H P N I A R B
S P R B R H P R O M I S E Q T B T H L N T
```

Find the answers on page 139

Quiz 6
IT'S A MIRACLE!
PART ONE

When the people of Israel saw the mighty works of the Lord, they sang a song of praise to Him. They honored Him for His greatness and strength and power. They called Him an awesome God.

LET'S LEARN ABOUT SOME OF THE MIRACLES FOUND IN THE OLD TESTAMENT.

1. **What did God tell Moses to hold over the Red Sea so the Israelites could go across? (Exodus 14:16)**
   a) a rock
   b) his hand
   c) a snake
   d) his staff

2. **How did the Israelites cross the Red Sea? (Exodus 14:22)**
   a) a boat appeared and they got on board
   b) they were able to swim very fast
   c) birds carried them across
   d) the water parted and they walked across on dry land

3. **Who was chasing the Israelites across the Red Sea? (Exodus 14:23)**
   a) the Egyptian army
   b) the Canaanites
   c) the Moabites
   d) a swarm of locusts

4. **Which prophet helped a widow sell olive oil? (see 2 Kings 4:1–7)**
   a) Elisha
   b) Elijah
   c) Samuel
   d) Moses

5. **How many jars did the widow fill with olive oil? (2 Kings 4:5–6)**
   a) one large jar
   b) 7
   c) 22
   d) all the jars her sons brought her

6. **Where did Elijah win a victory over the prophets of the false god Baal? (1 Kings 18:20–21)**
   a) Jericho
   b) Mount Sinai
   c) Mount Carmel
   d) the desert

7. **How many of Baal's prophets did Elijah challenge? (1 Kings 18:19)**
   a) 3
   b) 10
   c) 75
   d) 450

8. **How did Elijah light his altar when he challenged the prophets of Baal? (1 Kings 18:36–38)**
   a) he used a torch
   b) he lit a match
   c) he prayed
   d) he set up the altar close to a lightning storm

Find the answers on page 140

Make as many words as you
can out of the letters in

MIRACLE

_____   _____

_____   _____

_____   _____

_____   _____

_____   _____

_____   _____

_____   _____

_____   _____

_____   _____

CROSSWORD PUZZLE

ACROSS

3. Which false god were 450 prophets worshipping on Mount Carmel? (1 Kings 18:19)
4. God split the Red Sea in _____ so the people could walk across (Exodus 14:21)
5. Elisha told the widow to borrow jars from her _____ (2 Kings 4:3)
9. Which king did Elijah stand up against on Mount Carmel? (1 Kings 18:1)
11. How many sons did the widow who called out to Elisha have? (2 Kings 4:1)
12. One color of olive oil

DOWN

1. Elijah poured _____ on his altar before he prayed to God (1 Kings 18:33)
2. Who sent his army after Moses and the Israelites when they left Egypt? (Exodus 14:8)
6. Fire came down from _____ to burn up Elijah's altar (1 Kings 18:38)
7. The widow needed money to pay her _____ (2 Kings 4:7)
8. How many stones did Elijah use to rebuild the altar? (1 Kings 18:31)
10. The person who raised his staff over the Red Sea (Exodus 14:15–16)

Find the answers on page 140

WORD SEARCH
Can you find all the words?
Words may be forward, up-and-down, or diagonal.

ALTAR   ELISHA   OIL

ARMY   FIRE   OLIVE

DRY GROUND   JAR   PHARAOH

ELIJAH   MOSES   WIDOW

```
G B N D N M K P W S A R
H B C D W E L I S H A B D Q
D F O L I V E D W S Q O X M R N
Q F B M R T W S D H C X D Q S O G H
A B I W Q S X G H K L P M N R H G S W B
R M R W P H A R A O H R V N D N K S E B
M R E B Q L M D R Y G R O U N D R C M S
Y K N C S X Z W Q R W H N S D V J M B H
E L I J A H K D B X Q W H N K A W B
P T B L R W N M C S O Q K Q R M
K R T B N D M K Q B I Q M W
G A B M K B Z O X W L K
R G H Q D B D W Z B
D C W I D O W B
```

Find the answers on page 140

OLD TESTAMENT HEROES
PART TWO

Joshua, Esther, and Daniel were three brave people who loved and obeyed God. Their stories of bravery are found in the Old Testament.

USE YOUR BIBLE TO HELP YOU
ANSWER THE QUESTIONS BELOW.

1. **After Moses died, Joshua became the new leader of the Israelites. What did God tell Joshua to do? (Joshua 1:2)**
   a) go back to Egypt
   b) climb a mountain
   c) lead the Israelites across the Jordan River
   d) go on a picnic

2. **Why did God want the people to go into Canaan? (Exodus 6:8)**
   a) to enter the land God promised to Abraham
   b) to meet their new neighbors
   c) to have better food
   d) to see more animals

3. **What did God tell the people to place on the side of the river after they finished crossing it? (Joshua 4:1–3)**
   a) their shoes
   b) their backpacks
   c) a pile of twelve stones
   d) a bucket of water from the river

4. **What place of honor did Esther receive? (Esther 2:16–17)**
   a) she became a princess
   b) she became a queen
   c) she became the president
   d) she was adopted by the king

5. **How did God use Esther? (Esther 8:3–6)**
   a) she hid some spies
   b) she gave beauty treatments to her friends
   c) she saved the Jewish people from being killed
   d) she taught cooking lessons

6. **What king did Daniel work for?**
   (Daniel 6:1–2)
   a) King Henry
   b) King David
   c) King Herod
   d) King Darius

7. **Why was Daniel thrown in the lions' den?**
   (Daniel 6:10–12)
   a) he prayed to God when it was against the king's law
   b) the den needed to be cleaned
   c) the lions were hungry
   d) the king was jealous of Daniel

8. **Why didn't the lions hurt Daniel?**
   (Daniel 6:21–22)
   a) they were sleeping
   b) they didn't have any teeth
   c) they had just eaten a big meal
   d) God sent an angel to protect Daniel

Find the answers on page 141

MATCH THE HERO TO THEIR STORY

Which hero's story matches each picture on the right?

JOSHUA

ESTHER

DANIEL

NOAH

MOSES

ELIJAH

WIDOW

Find the answers on page 141

WORD SEARCH
Can you find all the words?
Words may be forward, backward, or up-and-down.

CROWN	HERO	PRAYED
DANIEL	HUNGRY	PROMISED LAND
DEN	LAW	RIVER
ESTHER	LEADER	ROAR

```
              M
            N K E
          R N E D K
        D O R N M T L
      C B A W R I V E R
    K W N R D O R D H N T
  B G D B L E A D E R Q N P
F P R O M I S E D L A N D D O
H T N T B N P T Y Q R W T M T H T
  G D W A L T H U N G R Y T P K
    K P R A Y E D D D A N M K
      N L N Q R R D K G D S
        D A N I E L M Q W
          N B D O R E H
            N W O R C
              C Q L
               H
```

Find the answers on page 141

CROSSWORD PUZZLE

ACROSS

4. What river did God's people have to cross? (Joshua 3:1)
5. God's people who wandered in the wilderness (Numbers 14:2)
6. Daniel prayed to God on his _____ (Daniel 6:10)
8. What king passed a law that the people had to pray only to him? (Daniel 6:7–9)
9. Who did Daniel only pray to? (Daniel 6:10)
10. The people Esther saved were _____ (Esther 8:3)

DOWN

1. Esther became a _____ (Esther 2:17)
2. God sent an _____ to protect Daniel (Daniel 6:22)
3. How many times a day did Daniel pray? (Daniel 6:10)
4. Who led the people after Moses died? (Joshua 1:1)
6. The person who rules a kingdom (Deuteronomy 17:15)
7. Daniel spent a night with these animals (Daniel 6:22)

Find the answers on page 142

Quiz 8
BE WISE

The Bible has many chapters and verses that show how God can help us make good decisions when we follow Him. Psalms and Proverbs are two of the "wisdom" books of the Bible.

**OPEN YOUR BIBLE IF YOU NEED
HELP WITH THE ANSWERS TO THE
FOLLOWING QUESTIONS.**

1. **What name is given to God in Psalm 23?**
   a) Friend
   b) Leader
   c) King
   d) Shepherd

2. **According to Psalm 33:12, what kind of nation does God bless?**
   a) a nation with a strong army
   b) a nation with rich people
   c) a nation whose God is the Lord
   d) a nation with cool flags

3. **According to Psalm 92:1, what is a good thing to do?**
   a) get good grades in school
   b) help your mom with the dishes
   c) praise God
   d) read good books

4. **What can help us when we are tempted to sin? (Psalm 119:11)**
   a) having good friends
   b) knowing God's word
   c) closing our eyes
   d) going for a walk

5. **What does Proverbs 3:5–6 tell us to do so that God will lead and direct our lives?**
   a) go to church on Sunday
   b) obey the 10 commandments
   c) be kind to your friends
   d) trust Him with all our heart

6. **How do we get wisdom and knowledge? (Proverbs 9:10)**
   a) by fearing and knowing God
   b) by reading the dictionary
   c) by getting enough sleep
   d) by watching TV

7. **According to Proverbs 17:22, what is good medicine?**
   a) a glass of milk
   b) fish oil
   c) a cheerful heart
   d) green tea

8. **What is better than having riches? (Proverbs 22:1)**
   a) having lots of friends
   b) having a good name (reputation)
   c) eating lots of vegetables
   d) winning a trophy

Find the answers on page 142

Find these 9 words in the puzzle box below and cross out the letters as you go. The letters of each word are connected in a row. BUT they may read in ANY direction!

FACTS   GRASP   LOGIC   RULER   WORDS
FEELING   KING   NEWS   SPEAK

L	O	R	D	W	I	C	S	D
O	M	M	O	U	T	I	H	K
F	E	E	L	I	N	G	N	O
S	W	S	S	L	R	O	P	E
D	T	W	P	U	G	L	S	W
E	E	C	L	E	U	N	A	O
N	D	E	A	E	A	R	R	R
S	R	T	A	F	N	K	G	D
K	I	N	G	D	I	N	G	S

STEP TWO

Copy the remaining letters, one by one—starting from top left, moving left to right—to each blank space below to discover the hidden words of this verse!

FOR THE ___ ___ ___ GRANTS ___ ___ ___ ___ ___ ___ !

FROM HIS ___ ___ ___ COME ___ ___ ___ ___ ___ ___ ___

AND ___ ___ ___ ___ ___ ___ ___ ___ ___ ___ ___ .

PROVERBS 2:6 NLT

WORD SEARCH
Can you find all the words?
Words may be forward, backward, or up-and-down.

BIBLE	KNOWLEDGE	SHEPHERD
BLESS	LORD	TRUST
GOOD	PRAISE	UNDERSTANDING
HEART	PROVERBS	WISDOM

```
K M C Z Q R O N S R B S D B R H E A R T H K
R W H U N D E R S T A N D I N G K L N N T Y
D T C M O D S I W C T F T R U S T M L Y K N
E L B I B Q W P K Q P R A I S E W D O M Q D
K N O W L E D G E T R P S H E P H E R D G B
P D W Q G H S O E R T S P Q T S F W D H R W
W M D B Q P R O V E R B S F S T M Q R X C H
M B S B N T T D T H G B L E S S W X C R N P
K L P W B R S C F W S D Q T Y D F X Z R M R
```

Find the answers on page 143

CROSSWORD PUZZLE

ACROSS

3. The Holy Spirit helps us to _____ God's Word (Job 32:8)
7. A person who takes care of sheep (Psalm 78:70–71)
8. Another word for "psalm" (Psalm 98:1)
10. Reading the Bible helps us to be _____ (Psalm 19:7)
11. Solomon wrote many wise sayings in the book of _____

DOWN

1. A person who leads other people (Psalm 48:14)
2. Telling God how wonderful He is (Psalm 150)
4. Who wrote many of the Psalms? (Psalm 72:20)
5. God wants us to _____ Him (Proverbs 3:5)
6. There are 31 of these in the book of Proverbs
9. What word describes God in Psalm 48:1?
10. Another name for the Bible is God's _____

Find the answers on page 143

Quiz 9
THE FIRST CHRISTMAS

Jesus came from His beautiful home in heaven to a humble place on earth. But God had a plan and purpose for sending His Son to earth. Jesus was the promised Messiah. He would forgive people of their sins and make them right with God.

WHAT DO YOU KNOW ABOUT THE FIRST CHRISTMAS WHEN JESUS WAS BORN?

1. **Where was Jesus born? (Luke 2:4–6)**
   a) Nazareth
   b) Bethlehem
   c) Galilee
   d) Jerusalem

2. **Who were Jesus's parents on earth? (Luke 1:27)**
   a) Zechariah and Elizabeth
   b) Abraham and Sarah
   c) Jacob and Rachel
   d) Joseph and Mary

3. **How did Jesus's parents find out they were going to have a baby? (Luke 1:28)**
   a) the king told them
   b) an angel shared the news
   c) they got a letter in the mail
   d) baby Jesus was dropped off on their doorstep

4. **Who did the angel first tell about Jesus's birth? (Luke 2:8–11)**
   a) shepherds
   b) King Herod
   c) wise men
   d) John the Baptist

5. **What appeared in the sky when Jesus was born? (Matthew 2:1–2)**
   a) fireworks
   b) lightning
   c) a bright star
   d) the Goodyear blimp

6. **Which of the following was not a gift the wise men brought to Jesus? (Matthew 2:11)**
   a) gold
   b) silver
   c) frankincense
   d) myrrh

7. **Where did baby Jesus sleep the night He was born? (Luke 2:6–7)**
   a) in a crib
   b) on a throne
   c) in a basket
   d) in a manger

8. **Who told the wise men he wanted to find baby Jesus? (Matthew 2:7-8)**
   a) King Xerxes
   b) King Herod
   c) King David
   d) King Darius

Find the answers on page 144

CROSSWORD PUZZLE

ACROSS

2. The angel who told Mary that she would have a baby (see Luke 1:26)
5. Where did Mary and Joseph go to register for the census? (Luke 2:4)
7. What did the wise men follow to find Jesus? (Matthew 2:9)
8. Joseph was a relative of King _____ (see Luke 2:4)
10. Jesus's relative, who was born shortly before Him (see Luke 1:57–60)
11. Mary wrapped Jesus in strips of _____ (Luke 2:12)

DOWN

1. Mary kept all these things like a treasure in her _____ (Luke 2:19)
3. An _____ told the shepherds that Jesus was born (Luke 2:8–9)
4. The king who wanted to hurt Jesus shortly after He was born (Matthew 2:16)
6. The wise men came from the _____ looking for baby Jesus (Matthew 2:1)
7. Jesus came to be our _____ (Luke 2:11)
9. There was no room for Mary and Joseph to stay at this place (Luke 2:7)

Find the answers on page 144

FINISH THE PICTURE

Complete the scene of the First Christmas below by drawing the stable, the star, and some of the visitors who came to meet baby Jesus (shepherds, animals, angels)

WORD SEARCH
Can you find all the words?
Words may be forward, backward, or up-and-down.

ANGELS	JESUS	SAVIOR
BETHLEHEM	JOSEPH	SHEPHERDS
HEROD	MANGER	STAR
INN	MARY	WISE MEN

```
R I M H M A R Y L P F V J E S U S B S G
T N C B E T H L E H E M S D B N S T T R
  N D G Q S X Z S H E P H E R D S G A
  B W I S E M E N N K E L B K T S D R
  S D O R E H K N G J O S E P H S M M
    N R O I V A S M E S S L E G N A
    H E R D S R M A N G E R H O
```

JESUS'S STORIES

Jesus often told stories that had a special meaning. Those stories are called parables. Sometimes people were confused by His stories, but Jesus helped His followers understand the parables.

USE YOUR BIBLE TO FIND THE ANSWERS TO THE QUESTIONS ABOUT JESUS'S PARABLES.

1. **Who was a "neighbor" to a Jewish man who was hurt by robbers? (Luke 10:30–37)**
   a) a Levite
   b) a priest
   c) a Samaritan
   d) an innkeeper

2. **Which of these was not "lost" in the three parables Jesus told in Luke 15?**
   a) a wagon
   b) a sheep
   c) a coin
   d) a man's son

3. **What does Jesus teach in the parable of the Pharisee and the tax collector? (Luke 18:10–14)**
   a) we need to pray out loud
   b) we need to be humble
   c) we need to be proud
   d) we need to be kind

4. **In the parable of the sower, what do the seeds stand for? (Mark 4:3–20)**
   a) wheat
   b) corn
   c) the word of God
   d) fertilizer

5. **How is a mustard seed like the Kingdom of God? (Mark 4:30–33)**
   a) it feeds a lot of people
   b) everyone likes mustard
   c) it grows quickly
   d) it's a tiny seed but grows into a large plant

6. In His parable of the lamp, what does Jesus say we should do? (Matthew 5:14–16)
   a) let our light shine for Jesus
   b) sing songs of praise
   c) invite our neighbors to church
   d) read good books

7. What did the wise man do before a big storm in one of Jesus's parables? (Matthew 7:24–27)
   a) he built a boat
   b) he built his house on sandy ground
   c) he built his house on a rock
   d) he built a tower

8. When do the angels in heaven rejoice? (Luke 15:8–10)
   a) when we read the Bible
   b) when people get married
   c) when we go to church
   d) when someone becomes a Christian

Find the answers on page 145

Help the shepherd find the lost sheep!

Start

End

Find the answer on page 145

WORD SEARCH
Can you find all the words?
Words may be forward, backward, or up-and-down.

CHRISTIAN	LIGHT	SAMARITAN
HEAVEN	MUSTARD	SEEDS
HUMBLE	REJOICE	SHINE
KINGDOM	ROCK	SOWER

```
G B N M K L P Y T R W S Q S H I N E M B
B D W T H G I L D O M G Q E H N T C L Y
T M U S T A R D L C R M N E B G P C E K
W R E J O I C E M K Q W G D D H G N X Z
P N C G R E L B M U H M T S B W Q B S X
S A M A R I T A N S H W X F G R E W O S
R T B D H E A V E N N R G K I N G D O M
B G R T B M C H R I S T I A N M K L P B
```

Find the answers on page 145

CROSSWORD PUZZLE

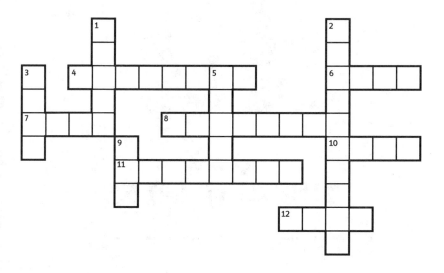

ACROSS

4. Many people _____ Jesus (Matthew 4:25)
6. The wise man built his house on this (Matthew 7:24)
7. Being a good neighbor means being _____ to others
8. Another name for the stories Jesus told (Matthew 13:34)
10. The size of a mustard seed (goes with "teeny"; see Mark 4:31)
11. The Samaritan was a good _____ (Luke 10:36–37)
12. What the foolish man built his house on (Matthew 7:26)

DOWN

1. The opposite of humble
2. People who believe in Jesus as their Savior
3. One of the books of the Bible where Jesus's parables are found
5. Jesus taught people while He lived on _____
9. In Luke 15:4–6, how many sheep were lost?

Find the answers on page 146

THE DISCIPLES

Jesus had twelve followers called "disciples." They saw Jesus perform many miracles. Most of Jesus's disciples were committed to following Him, even when it was hard to understand His teaching.

WHAT DO YOU KNOW ABOUT JESUS'S CLOSEST FOLLOWERS?
You can use your Bible to help you find the answers to the questions below.

1. **Who were the first four disciples of Jesus? (Matthew 4:18–21)**
   a) Peter, Andrew, James, and John
   b) Judas, Thomas, Thaddeus, and Philip
   c) Levi, Simon, Bartholomew, and Peter
   d) Peter, Andrew, Bartholomew, and Judas

2. **What were the first four disciples doing when Jesus told them to follow Him? (Matthew 4:18–21)**

   a) eating dinner

   b) going to the temple

   c) fishing

   d) sleeping

3. **What job did Levi, also known as Matthew, have before he became a disciple? (Luke 5:27–28)**

   a) carpenter

   b) priest

   c) scribe

   d) tax collector

4. **What was Peter's name before Jesus renamed him? (John 1:42)**

   a) Abram

   b) Simon

   c) Joseph

   d) John

5. **Which disciple turned Jesus over to His enemies? (Luke 22:47–48)**

   a) James

   b) John

   c) Philip

   d) Judas

6. **Which disciple walked on the water toward Jesus? (Matthew 14:29)**
   a) Thomas
   b) John
   c) Peter
   d) James

7. **Which disciple found the young boy whose lunch was used to miraculously feed 5,000 people? (John 6:8–9)**
   a) James
   b) Andrew
   c) Peter
   d) John

8. **Which disciple said he had to see the holes in Jesus's hands and side to believe He had risen from the dead? (John 20:24–25)**
   a) Thomas
   b) Judas
   c) Bartholomew
   d) Andrew

Find the answers on page 146

CODED MESSAGE

Use the key below to match the symbols of Jesus's message to letters to break the code!

Find the answer on page 146

CROSSWORD PUZZLE

ACROSS

6. The name of Peter's brother (Matthew 4:18)
7. What was another name of Judas, who betrayed Jesus? (Mark 3:19)
8. How many disciples did Jesus select to follow Him? (Matthew 10:1)
9. When Jesus called the first disciples, what were they casting into the sea? (Matthew 4:20)
10. James's brother, who was also a disciple (Matthew 4:21)
11. Peter said _____ times that he didn't know Jesus (Mark 14:30)

DOWN

1. Levi was also called _____ (see Matthew 9:9 and Luke 5:27)
2. Thomas said he had to see the marks of the _____ in Jesus's hands (John 20:25)
3. Peter walked on the _____ toward Jesus (Matthew 14:29)
4. John and _____ saw the empty tomb after Jesus rose from the dead (John 20:3)
5. Who replaced Judas after he betrayed Jesus? (Acts 1:24–26)
8. Jesus gave James and John the nickname "sons of _____" (Mark 3:17)

Find the answers on page 147

WORD SEARCH
Can you find all the words?
Words may be forward, backward, or up-and-down.

BROTHERS	HANDS	TAX COLLECTOR
DISCIPLE	JOHN	THUNDER
FISHERMEN	NETS	TWELVE
FOLLOW	PETER	WATER

```
Q N R G P E T E R K N D B W R S T P D W
H B D G P T A X C O L L E C T O R M N B
A D B W T W E L V E H K D N H O J B E M
N M D D I S C I P L E M W N D S Q N T S
D B R B R O T H E R S H A M Q P K L S H
S W L L Q W O L L O F H T W P Q H R S G
F M F G Q V Z X F I S H E R M E N N F H
R E D N U H T M N P L K R M H R P T E P
```

Find the answers on page 147

Quiz 12
IT'S A MIRACLE!
PART TWO

While Jesus was on earth, He performed many miracles. He healed the sick, fed thousands of people with a boy's lunch, and raised people from the dead. His miracles not only showed that He wanted to help people, they also showed that Jesus was the Son of God.

WHAT DO YOU KNOW ABOUT SOME OF JESUS'S MIRACLES?
The Bible verses will help you find the answers.

1. **What was the first miracle that Jesus performed? (John 2:1–11)**
   a) He parted the Red Sea
   b) He turned stones into bread
   c) He turned water into wine
   d) He healed a sick woman

2. **What miracle did Jesus do to help His disciples? (Luke 5:4–7)**
   a) He sent wind for their sailboat
   b) He helped them see in the dark
   c) He stopped the rain
   d) He helped them catch a net full of fish

3. **What miracle did Jesus perform in the city of Nain? (Luke 7:11–17)**
   a) He fed 3,000 people
   b) He raised a widow's son from the dead
   c) He healed a blind man
   d) He flew

4. **What did Jesus do in Mark 4:35–41 that amazed His disciples?**
   a) He walked on the water
   b) He caught fish without a net
   c) He calmed a storm
   d) He made pizza

5. **How did a paralyzed man's friends get him to Jesus for a miraculous healing? (Mark 2:1–5)**
   a) they let him down through the roof
   b) they brought him on a wagon
   c) they floated him on a raft
   d) they broke through a door

6. **What did Jesus use to feed 5,000 men and their wives and children? (Matthew 14:13–21)**
   a) a handful of grain
   b) seven fig cakes and seven apples
   c) a large basket of grapes
   d) five loaves of bread and two fish

7. **When Jesus healed ten men with leprosy, how many came back to thank Him? (Luke 17:11–19)**
   a) all ten
   b) nine
   c) three
   d) only one

8. **Who were the sisters of Lazarus, a man Jesus raised from the dead? (John 11:1)**
   a) Leah and Rachel
   b) Mary and Martha
   c) Mary and Elizabeth
   d) Ruth and Naomi

Find the answers on page 148

CONNECT THE DOTS

Connect the dots below to create a picture
of one of Jesus's many miracles.

WORD SEARCH
Can you find all the words?
Words may be forward, backward, or up-and-down.

BREAD	MARTHA	PEOPLE
FISH	MARY	SAILBOAT
HEALED	MIRACLE	STORM
LAZARUS	NAIN	TEN

```
D B M K L S A I L B O A T G R H N V J M
B R D S W R T P K H S I F M N A I N M A
N E K S Q N Q T S M P L T D G R K B C R
N A Z M I R A C L E M P R N S T Q B D Y
D D K L A Z A R U S N P L S M E D S B Q
P G H S T O R M N B L Y G P B N K L N O
D B N G H P T R T M A R T H A Q D J T Y
H B E H E A L E D M H E L P O E P R D J
```

Find the answers on page 148

CROSSWORD PUZZLE

ACROSS

4. The name of a man Jesus raised from the dead (John 11:43–44)
8. At what event did Jesus perform his first miracle? (John 2:1–2)
9. Jesus healed ten men. How many men said thank you? (Luke 17:17–18)
10. How many sisters did Lazarus have? (see John 11:5)
11. How many jars did Jesus tell the servants to fill? (John 2:6–7)
12. Jesus fed 5,000 _____ and their families (Matthew 14:21)

DOWN

1. People who cannot see are _____
2. What did Jesus turn into wine? (see John 2:7)
3. In the city of Nain, Jesus brought the son of a _____ back to life (see Luke 7:12)
5. Jesus spoke to the wind and waves to calm a _____ (see Mark 4:35–39)
6. A disease that causes sores on the skin
7. Where did Lazarus and his sisters live? (John 11:1)

Find the answers on page 148

Quiz 13
TEACH US TO PRAY

Prayer is talking to God. We can pray to thank God. We can pray when we're sad or scared, or to ask for things we need. Prayer can be powerful. Sometimes when we pray, God will do things that seem impossible. Jesus taught His disciples how to pray.

WHAT DO YOU KNOW ABOUT HIS SPECIAL PRAYER, CALLED "THE LORD'S PRAYER"?

You can use your Bible to help you find answers to the questions below.

1. **When Jesus began His prayer, He called God our Father in _____. (Matthew 6:9)**
   a) heaven
   b) the sky
   c) outer space
   d) the temple

2. How are we supposed to treat God's name? (see Matthew 6:9)
   a) we should never say it out loud
   b) we should only call God "Lord"
   c) we should honor His name as holy
   d) we should say it however we want

3. How much food or bread should we pray for each day? (Matthew 6:11)
   a) enough for the whole year
   b) enough for our whole lives
   c) enough for one week
   d) enough for the day

4. We should pray for God's _____ to come. (Matthew 6:10)
   a) punishment
   b) kingdom
   c) angels
   d) help

5. When we disobey God, what should we ask Him to do? (Matthew 6:12)
   a) punish us
   b) forgive our sins
   c) look the other way
   d) bless us

6. **Who are we supposed to forgive? (Matthew 6:12)**
   a) people who apologize to us
   b) only people who are our friends
   c) other Christians
   d) anyone who does wrong to us

7. **What should we ask God to keep us from? (Matthew 6:13)**
   a) mean people
   b) danger
   c) temptation
   d) getting hurt

8. **Whose "will"—or whose plans and desires—should we pray for? (see Matthew 6:10)**
   a) God's
   b) our own
   c) our parents'
   d) our teachers'

Find the answers on page 149

FILL IN THE BLANKS
Try to fill in as many blanks as you can
without looking at your Bible!

Our _____ in heaven,

Hallowed be Your _____'.

Your _____ come.

Your _____ be done

On _____ as it is in _____ .

Give us this day our daily _____.

And _____ us our debts,

As we _____ our debtors.

And do not lead us into temptation,

But deliver us from the _____ one.

For Yours is the _____ and the

_____ and the _____ forever.

Amen.

Matthew 6:9–13 NKJV

Find the answers on page 149

CROSSWORD PUZZLE

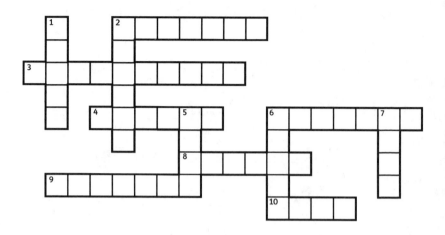

ACROSS

2. We should pray for God to _____ our sins (Matthew 6:12)
3. Wanting to do something you know is wrong (Matthew 6:13)
4. God sees when you pray and will _____ you (Matthew 6:6)
6. Who we ask God to save us from (Matthew 6:13)
8. God will forgive us if we forgive _____ (see Matthew 6:14)
9. We ask God for His _____ to come (Matthew 6:10)
10. God's name is _____ (Psalm 105:3)

DOWN

1. Jesus said we should ask God to give us daily _____ (Matthew 6:11)
2. What does Jesus call God in the beginning of His prayer? (Matthew 6:9)
5. A place you can go when you pray (Matthew 6:6)
6. We pray that God will have His way in heaven and on _____ (Matthew 6:10)
7. Your Father knows what you _____ before you ask Him (Matthew 6:8)

Find the answers on page 149

WORD SEARCH
Can you find all the words?
Words may be forward, backward, or up-and-down.

BREAD   FATHER   KINGDOM

DAILY   FORGIVE   NEED

DOOR   HEAVEN   PRAYER

EARTH   HOLY   TEMPTATION

```
Q N E E D L W D T F G S R T
G H K M N B R E A D H Q K B D D
G B H Q W D S N M O D G N I K N A B
D F G W Q P R A Y E R B W M T L T I D B
N E V A E H H M R G R H D B K T X L T N
F M F O R G I V E W Q O M N K X T Y V T
D S R R O O D B C D W L N B G R W B X C
F A T H E R N B D Q Y Q E A R T H W
G T M V L R C K E E D N W S B M
N T E M P T A T I O N R S M
```

Find the answers on page 150

JESUS'S DEATH AND RESURRECTION

Jesus had many followers when He lived on earth, but some people were against Him. He was nailed to a cross and died the death of a criminal. But that's not the end of the story! Jesus came back to life and now lives with God the Father in heaven.

WHAT DO YOU KNOW ABOUT JESUS'S DEATH AND RESURRECTION?

1. **What did Judas receive from the priests when he agreed to lead them to Jesus? (Matthew 26:15)**
   - **a)** three gold coins
   - **b)** ten copper coins
   - **c)** thirty pieces of silver
   - **d)** gold, frankincense, and myrrh

2. **Where did Jesus go to pray shortly before He was arrested? (Matthew 26:36)**
   a) the town of Bethlehem
   b) a place called Gethsemane
   c) the Sea of Galilee
   d) the Mount of Olives

3. **Which disciple said he did not know Jesus? (Matthew 26:69–70)**
   a) Judas
   b) Thomas
   c) John
   d) Peter

4. **What did soldiers place on Jesus's head as they made fun of Him? (Matthew 27:29)**
   a) a paper crown
   b) a crown made with thorns
   c) a metal helmet
   d) a hat made from wool

5. **Who was told to carry Jesus's cross? (Matthew 27:32)**
   a) Simon from Cyrene
   b) Simon Peter
   c) John, the disciple
   d) Jesus's brothers

6. **What happened at noon while Jesus hung on the cross? (Matthew 27:45)**

    a) the disciples ran away

    b) the robbers next to Jesus died

    c) the sky became dark

    d) a rainbow appeared in the sky

7. **When they saw the earthquake and all that happened while Jesus died on the cross, what did some of the guards say? (Matthew 27:54)**

    a) "God is punishing us!"

    b) "Jesus was only a man."

    c) "Jesus truly was the Son of God!"

    d) "We must find a tomb for Him."

8. **What did an angel tell the women who went to Jesus's tomb? (Matthew 28:5–7)**

    a) "Jesus is in heaven."

    b) "Jesus has risen from the dead."

    c) "Jesus is at the temple."

    d) "Jesus went to Bethlehem."

Find the answers on page 150

FINISH THE PICTURE

Using the grid provided, draw the reflection of the image shown to complete the picture.

CROSSWORD PUZZLE

ACROSS

1. What color robe was put on Jesus to mock Him? (Mark 15:17)
3. Jesus told His disciples that he would _____ be with them (Matthew 28:20)
7. About how many followers saw Jesus after He rose from the dead? (1 Corinthians 15:6)
9. How many other men were crucified with Jesus? (Matthew 27:38)
10. The stories about Jesus are written so that people will _____ that He is the Son of God (John 20:31)

DOWN

1. What leader said Jesus hadn't done anything wrong? (John 19:4)
2. What was the name of the place where Jesus was crucified? (Mark 15:22)
4. When Jesus was on the cross He said He was _____ (John 19:28)
5. What bad guy was set free instead of Jesus? (Mark 15:15)
6. Where could Jesus's friends find Him after He rose from the dead? (Matthew 28:7)
8. Who owned the tomb that was used for Jesus's body? (Matthew 27:57–60)
11. When Thomas saw that Jesus was alive he said, "My _____ and my God!" (John 20:28)

Find the answers on page 150

WORD SEARCH
Can you find all the words?
Words may be forward, backward, or up-and-down.

ANGEL   EARTHQUAKE   SILVER
CROSS   GUARD   STONE
CROWN   PRIESTS   TOMB
DARK   ROBBERS   WOMEN

```
          U B L A R H P J
          Z E N O T S N M
          R L Y J A S H E
          N S I L V E R L
  K E A R T H Q U A K E O T R Q K U H
  P X G N S S O R C H M B T W I L M E
  Y M C I H S O W N W L B E R Y K A J
  L V P R I E S T S H U E L S N I T O
  I T E O B A I F L E T R U T W S M C
  Q S P A W O H G N Q R S F S H U T W
          B W O M E N J C
          C Z A N G E L I
          F D C R O W N T
          M H U B W O D S
          E Q G U A R D H
          X T O M B R L K
          H A N D W E G O
          V Y E P O K N W
          G D A R K L O M
          E J U S M R Q Y
```

Find the answers on page 151

THE HOLY SPIRIT

After Jesus went back to heaven, the Holy Spirit came to the disciples. He helped them do things they could not do before. The Holy Spirit was the Helper Jesus had promised. The Holy Spirit is our helper too.

HOW MANY QUESTIONS CAN YOU ANSWER ABOUT THE HOLY SPIRIT?

1. **What did Jesus say the disciples would receive from the Holy Spirit? (Acts 1:8)**
   a) doves
   b) power
   c) money
   d) friends

2. **When the Holy Spirit came into the room where the disciples were, what did it sound like? (Acts 2:2)**
   a) a freight train   c) a strong wind
   b) a bus   d) a lion's roar

3. **What did the disciples see above each others' heads when they received the Holy Spirit? (Acts 2:3)**
   a) small flames of fire
   b) golden crowns
   c) white doves
   d) butterflies

4. **What ability did the Holy Spirit give to the believers? (Acts 2:4)**
   a) they could run fast
   b) they could go without eating
   c) they could fly
   d) they could speak in different languages

5. **What were the other people talking about after they received the Holy Spirit? (Acts 2:11)**
   a) Roman leaders
   b) the great wonders of God
   c) the Olympics
   d) the weather

6. **Which disciple tried to explain to the people what was happening? (Acts 2:14)**
   a) James
   b) Matthew
   c) Peter
   d) John

7. **How could the other people in the crowd receive the Holy Spirit? (Acts 2:38)**
   a) they could ask the disciples
   b) they could go to the Temple
   c) they could climb the Mount of Olives
   d) they could turn away from their sins and be baptized

8. **What does the Holy Spirit do when we pray? (Romans 8:26)**
   a) He keeps us awake
   b) He sings
   c) He prays to God for us
   d) He flies around heaven

Find the answers on page 151

CROSSWORD PUZZLE

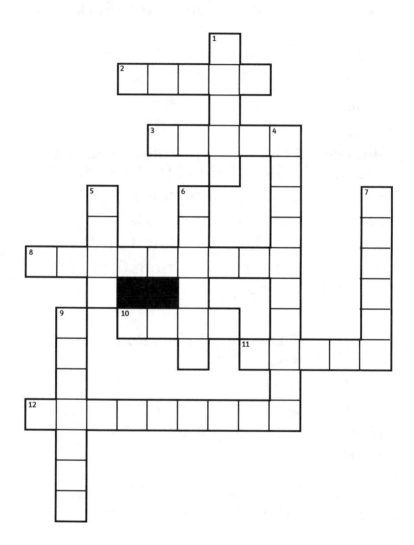

ACROSS

2. What did the Holy Spirit give to the disciples? (Acts 1:8)
3. The Holy Spirit is also called the Spirit of _____ (John 16:13)
8. People were surprised to hear the disciples speaking in different _____ (Acts 2:8)
10. What Old Testament prophet said that the Holy Spirit would come? (Acts 2:16–17)
11. When we pray, the Holy Spirit _____ for us (Romans 8:26)
12. The day the Holy Spirit came is called _____ (Acts 2:1)

DOWN

1. Who told the disciples they would receive a Helper? (John 14:9–17)
4. Who lives within us when we become Christians? (2 Timothy 1:14)
5. What did it sound like when the Holy Spirit came into the room? (Acts 2:2)
6. Where did Jesus go before the Holy Spirit came to earth? (Acts 1:11)
7. What appeared over the heads of the disciples when the Holy Spirit came? (Acts 2:3)
9. What did Jesus call His disciples when He knew He would soon be leaving them? (John 15:15)

Find the answers on page 152

Make as many words as you can out of the letters in

HOLY SPIRIT

_____   _____

_____   _____

_____   _____

_____   _____

_____   _____

_____   _____

_____   _____

_____   _____

WORD SEARCH
Can you find all the words?
Words may be forward, backward, or diagonal.

CHRISTIAN   HELPER   POWER

DISCIPLES   HOLY   SPIRIT

FLAMES   JESUS   TRUTH

FRIENDS   LANGUAGE   WIND

```
D H K M R H T U R T S N V J E S U S Q W
G W K L D S Z W C B P O W E R T L S Z M
Q M I K N D S E M A L F M W H P T N T Q
B D H N Q W F R I E N D S D W O P L N V
D X C B D M K S P I R I T H W L L B V S
W B Q D I S C I P L E S W N Q B H Y N L
R E P L E H M K H C H R I S T I A N N B
M N B L A N G U A G E M W P T L J S Z Q
```

Find the answers on page 152

NEW TESTAMENT HEROES

Many people followed Jesus, and they were all important. We can read the stories of some of Jesus's followers in the Bible. These people were very brave and did some amazing things. They weren't perfect, but God used them as a part of His plan.

WHAT DO YOU KNOW ABOUT THE NEW TESTAMENT'S HEROES AND HOW THEY HELPED TO SPREAD THE GOOD NEWS ABOUT JESUS?

1. **What did John the Baptist announce in the wilderness? (Luke 3:2–4)**
   a) "Prepare the way of the Lord!"
   b) "Today, in the City of David, a Savior has been born!"
   c) "He is risen!"
   d) "Love your neighbor as yourself."

2. **What well-known person did John the Baptist baptize? (Mark 1:9)**
   a) Peter
   b) Paul
   c) Jesus
   d) Timothy

3. **What special thing did the apostle John see with Peter and James? (Mark 9:2–4)**
   a) the Nile River split in two
   b) the temple being rebuilt
   c) Jesus in bright clothes, talking with Moses and Elijah
   d) the wise men bringing gifts to Jesus

4. **Where did Jesus first speak to the apostle Paul? (Acts 9:3–5)**
   a) in Bethlehem
   b) at Golgotha
   c) the Sea of Galilee
   d) the road to Damascus

5. **What was Paul's other name? (Acts 13:9)**
   a) Simon
   b) Saul
   c) Stephen
   d) Samson

6. **What great thing did Peter do in a town called Joppa? (Acts 9:40–41)**

   a) raised a woman from the dead

   b) walked on the water

   c) fed several thousand people

   d) healed a blind man

7. **How did Peter escape from prison? (Acts 12:7–9)**

   a) an earthquake opened the door

   b) an angel rescued him

   c) Paul snuck him out

   d) his friends dug a hole into his cell

8. **Where did John write the book of Revelation? (Revelation 1:9–11)**

   a) Egypt

   b) Jerusalem

   c) Athens

   d) the island of Patmos

Find the answers on page 153

MATCH THE HERO TO HIS STORY

Which hero matches each description on the right?

PETER

JOHN

PAUL

JOHN THE
BAPTIST

LAZARUS

ANDREW

MATTHEW

THOMAS

TIMOTHY

Paul's "son in
the faith"

Peter's brother

Jesus raised him
from the dead

writer of the
first Gospel

asked to see the
holes in Jesus's
hands

writer of
Revelation

walked on water
with Jesus

lived in the
wilderness

was temporarily
blinded by God

Find the answers on page 153

CROSSWORD PUZZLE

ACROSS

2. The name of Peter's brother (Matthew 4:18)
4. The last word of Revelation, written by the disciple John (Revelation 22:21)
5. The name of Paul's "son in the faith" (1 Timothy 1:2)
7. Peter stayed with this man after God gave him an important vision (Acts 10:22–23)
11. Peter told people to repent and be _____ after the Holy Spirit came at Pentecost (Acts 2:38)
12. John was known as the disciple whom Jesus _____ (John 19:26)

DOWN

1. The name of the disciple John's brother (Matthew 4:21)
3. The mother of John the Baptist (Luke 1:57–63)
6. Paul said he could do all things through Christ who gives him _____ (Philippians 4:13)
8. Paul survived this three times (2 Corinthians 11:25)
9. John the Baptist baptized with _____ (Luke 3:16)
10. The king who put John the Baptist in prison (Matthew 14:3)

Find the answers on page 153

WORD SEARCH
Can you find all the words?
Words may be forward, backward, or up-and-down.

BAPTIZE
DAMASCUS
LOCUSTS
PATMOS

PILLAR
PREPARE
REVELATION
ROCK

SAUL
SHIPWRECK
SIMON
ZEBEDEE

```
S M N L O C U S T S B Q R T P K C D S R
A H W X D S B A P T I Z E G K P B M T O
U K B N O I T A L E V E R H G T N W T C
L B D F G P D A M A S C U S L N S X N K
H S H I P W R E C K M N S H P T N X S T
N O M I S B D G E E D E B E Z K H M R P
B H D P R E P A R E M B Q P I L L A R Q
H B Q N R P T P A T M O S T L N N T S D
```

Find the answers on page 154

Quiz 17
LOVE

Jesus came to earth to show us how much God loves us. He taught people how to love God and how to love each other. God used some of Jesus's followers to write about love in the Bible so we can learn about God's love too.

HOW MANY QUESTIONS ABOUT LOVE CAN YOU ANSWER?

1. **What did Jesus say is the first great commandment? (Matthew 22:37–38)**
   a) obey your parents
   b) eat your vegetables
   c) don't tell lies
   d) love God with all your heart, soul, and mind

2. **What did Jesus say is the second great commandment? (Matthew 22:39)**
   a) go to church every week
   b) listen to Christian music
   c) love your neighbor as yourself
   d) drink plenty of water

3. **What are people like if they do not have love? (1 Corinthians 13:1)**
   a) a barking dog
   b) a clanging cymbal
   c) a honking horn
   d) a wailing siren

4. **Which of the following words describe what love is? (1 Corinthians 13:4)**
   a) patient and kind
   b) nice and clean
   c) soft and warm
   d) sweet and sour

5. **Where does the Bible say love comes from? (1 John 4:7)**
   a) our grandparents
   b) our parents
   c) the angels
   d) God

6. **What does God call us because He loves us so much? (1 John 3:1)**
   a) Christians
   b) the church
   c) His children
   d) His helpers

7. **What should we do because God loves us? (1 John 4:11)**
   a) jump up and down
   b) shout "Amen!"
   c) love other people
   d) sit still and fold our hands

8. **How long will God's love last? (Psalm 136:1)**
   a) as long as we obey Him
   b) as long as we love Him
   c) as long as we are good
   d) forever

Find the answers on page 154

CONNECT THE DOTS

Connect the dots below to see a very important message!

CROSSWORD PUZZLE

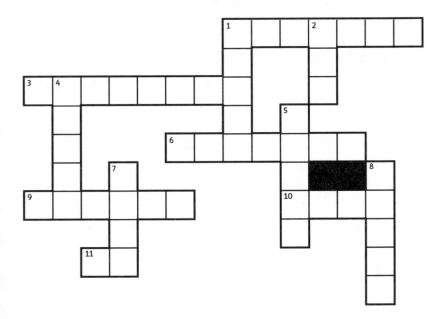

ACROSS

1. One way to show our love is to _____ others (Ephesians 4:32)
3. Jesus tells us to love our _____ (Matthew 22:39)
6. What can separate us from God's love? (see Romans 8:38–39)
9. Who died for us because of God's love? (Romans 5:8)
10. What is greater than faith and hope? (1 Corinthians 13:13)
11. We love others because God loves _____ (1 John 4:19)

DOWN

1. Loving God is the _____ great commandment (Matthew 22:37–38)
2. Who is love? (1 John 4:16)
4. God's love fills the _____ (Psalm 33:5)
5. What can we read to learn about God's love?
7. Because God loves us He forgives our _____ (1 John 1:9)
8. We should love God with all our _____ (Deuteronomy 6:5)

Find the answers on page 154

WORD SEARCH
Can you find all the words?
Words may be forward or backward.

CHILDREN	GOD	MIND
COMMANDMENT	HEART	NEIGHBOR
CYMBAL	KIND	PATIENT
FOREVER	LOVE	SOUL

```
          I L O                    K E L
        B E V J A                G O D S Q
      D V M I N D S            M C N T H L Y
    V D B T U H S A J        Y P H E A R T O E
    S C E V O L F R T H F M A O I R G U D S
  K R E A T S R K P K C H I L D R E N B N L H
  C Y M B A L F C W O B S A N H N B M T H H B
  X D S R O B H G I E N S M E R H K W C E X N
  O H C W I H D A E B O S G F O R E V E R M S
    N H C O M M A N D M E N T A H T R V C N
      R F S D W P L K J H G D S N K Q D B
        D R B E O I D S O U L T H P L O
          H Y H G B N T W D B N M T H
          H G B P A T I E N T D S
            B D R F A C H T B T
            W D N I K T H G
              C B N R T D
                R L W U
                  C D
```

Find the answers on page 155

FRUIT OF THE SPIRIT

Jesus promised that He would send His Holy Spirit to give power to His followers. With the Holy Spirit's strength, Christians would be able to face hard situations. The Holy Spirit gives Christians gifts—called "fruit"—to help them obey God.

WHAT DO YOU KNOW ABOUT THE FRUIT OF THE SPIRIT?

1. **How many good things are listed as the fruit of the Spirit? (Galatians 5:22–23)**
   a) three
   b) seven
   c) nine
   d) twelve

2. Which of these is not part of the fruit of the Spirit? (Galatians 5:22–23)
   a) joy
   b) selfishness
   c) love
   d) self-control

3. Which of these is not listed as the fruit of the Spirit? (Galatians 5:22–23)
   a) giving money to church
   b) peace
   c) patience
   d) kindness

4. The apostle Paul says there is no _____ that says the fruit of the Spirit is wrong. (Galatians 5:22–23)
   a) book
   b) person
   c) law
   d) king

5. What is the opposite of living life by God's Spirit? (Galatians 5:16–17)
   a) doing whatever we want, including sin
   b) doing what our parents tell us to do
   c) helping a friend who is hurt
   d) being a good listener

6. **When we live by the Spirit, what does Paul say we shouldn't be? (Galatians 5:26)**
   a) sleepy
   b) hyper
   c) frustrated
   d) conceited, or proud

7. **We have life in the Spirit because Jesus made us _____. (Galatians 5:1)**
   a) alive
   b) free
   c) clean
   d) happy

8. **What does Paul say we should use our freedom in the Spirit for? (Galatians 5:13)**
   a) making lots of money
   b) traveling the world
   c) singing solos at church
   d) serving each other, in love

Find the answers on page 155

COLOR BY NUMBER
How many hidden fruits can you find?

1=Red   2=Orange   3=Yellow   4=Green   5=Purple   6=Brown   7=Black

```
0 0 0 0 0 0 0 0 0 0 0 0 0 0 0 0 0 0 0 0 0 0 0 0 0 0 0 0 0 0 0
0 0 0 0 0 0 0 0 0 4 0 0 0 0 0 0 0 0 0 0 0 0 0 0 0 0 0 0 0 0 0
0 0 0 0 0 0 0 0 4 0 0 0 0 0 0 0 0 0 0 0 0 0 0 0 0 0 0 0 0 0 0
0 0 0 0 0 0 4 4 4 4 4 0 0 0 0 0 0 0 6 0 0 0 0 0 0 0 0 0 0 0 0
0 0 0 0 0 0 4 1 4 1 4 0 0 0 0 0 0 3 0 0 0 0 4 0 0 0 0 0 0 0 0
0 0 0 0 0 4 1 1 1 1 1 4 0 0 0 0 0 3 0 0 0 4 4 0 0 0 0 0 0 0 0
0 0 0 0 0 0 1 1 1 1 1 0 0 0 0 0 3 3 0 0 0 4 0 4 0 0 0 0 0 0 0
0 0 0 0 0 0 1 1 1 1 1 0 0 0 0 3 3 3 0 0 0 4 0 0 4 0 0 0 0 0 0
0 0 0 0 0 0 0 1 1 1 0 0 0 0 3 3 3 0 0 0 4 0 0 0 4 0 0 0 0 0 0
0 0 0 0 0 0 0 0 1 0 0 0 0 3 3 3 3 0 0 0 4 0 0 0 0 4 0 0 0 0 0
0 0 0 0 4 0 0 0 0 0 0 0 3 3 3 3 3 0 0 0 4 0 0 0 0 4 0 0 0 0 0
0 0 4 0 4 0 4 0 0 6 3 3 3 3 3 3 0 0 0 4 0 0 0 0 4 0 0 0 0 0 0
0 0 4 4 4 4 4 4 0 0 3 3 3 0 0 0 0 0 0 4 0 0 0 1 1 0 0 0 0 0 0
0 4 4 4 4 4 4 4 4 0 0 0 0 0 0 0 0 0 0 1 1 0 0 1 1 1 1 0 0 0 0
0 4 0 4 4 4 4 0 4 0 0 0 6 0 0 0 0 1 1 1 1 0 1 1 1 1 0 0 0 0 0
0 0 0 4 4 4 0 0 0 0 2 2 2 2 2 0 0 1 1 1 1 0 0 1 0 0 0 0 0 0 0
0 0 3 6 3 6 3 0 0 2 2 2 2 2 2 2 0 0 1 1 0 0 0 0 0 0 0 0 0 0 0
0 3 3 6 6 3 6 3 0 2 2 2 2 2 2 2 0 0 0 0 0 0 0 0 0 0 0 0 0 0 0
0 6 6 3 3 6 3 6 0 2 2 2 2 2 2 2 0 0 0 0 0 0 0 0 0 0 0 0 0 0 0
0 3 6 6 3 6 3 3 0 2 2 2 2 2 2 2 0 0 0 3 3 3 3 0 0 0 0 0 0 0 0
0 3 6 3 6 6 3 6 0 0 2 2 2 2 2 0 0 0 3 3 3 3 3 3 0 0 0 0 0 0 0
0 6 3 3 6 3 3 3 0 0 0 0 0 0 0 0 0 3 3 3 3 3 3 3 3 0 0 0 0 0 0
0 3 6 6 3 6 3 6 0 0 0 4 0 0 0 0 3 3 3 3 3 3 3 3 3 3 0 0 0 0 0
0 3 3 6 6 3 6 3 0 0 0 4 4 4 0 0 3 3 3 3 3 3 3 3 3 3 0 0 0 0 0
0 0 6 3 6 3 6 0 0 0 0 4 4 4 0 0 0 3 3 3 3 3 3 3 3 0 0 0 0 0 0
0 0 0 0 0 0 0 0 0 0 0 4 0 0 0 0 0 0 0 0 0 3 3 3 3 3 0 0 0 0 0
0 0 0 4 4 4 0 0 1 1 1 1 1 0 0 0 0 0 0 0 0 0 0 0 0 0 0 0 0 0 0
0 0 4 1 1 1 0 1 1 1 1 1 1 1 0 0 0 0 6 0 0 0 0 0 0 6 0 0 0 0 0
0 4 1 7 1 7 0 1 1 1 1 1 1 1 0 0 6 0 0 0 0 5 5 5 5 5 0 0 0 0 0
0 4 1 1 7 1 0 1 1 1 1 1 1 1 0 0 6 0 0 0 0 5 5 5 5 5 5 5 0 0 0
0 4 1 7 1 7 0 1 1 1 1 1 1 1 0 4 4 4 0 0 5 5 5 5 5 5 5 0 0 0 0
0 4 1 1 7 1 0 0 1 1 1 1 1 0 0 4 4 4 0 0 5 5 5 5 5 5 5 0 0 0 0
0 4 1 7 1 7 0 0 0 0 0 0 0 0 4 4 4 4 4 0 0 5 5 5 5 5 0 0 0 0 0
0 0 4 1 1 1 0 0 0 0 0 0 0 0 4 4 4 4 4 4 4 0 0 0 0 0 0 0 0 0 0
0 0 0 4 4 4 0 0 0 0 0 0 0 0 4 4 4 4 4 4 4 0 0 0 0 0 0 0 0 0 0
0 0 0 0 0 0 0 0 0 0 0 0 0 0 4 4 4 4 4 4 4 0 0 0 0 0 0 0 0 0 0
0 0 0 0 0 0 0 0 0 0 0 0 0 0 0 4 4 4 4 4 4 0 0 0 0 0 0 0 0 0 0
0 0 0 0 0 0 0 0 0 0 0 0 0 0 0 0 4 4 3 4 4 0 0 0 0 0 0 0 0 0 0
0 0 0 0 0 0 0 0 0 0 0 0 0 0 0 0 0 0 0 0 0 0 0 0 0 0 0 0 0 0 0
```

WORD SEARCH
Can you find all the words?
Words may be forward, backward, or up-and-down.

FAITHFULNESS   GOODNESS   PATIENCE

FREE   JOY   PEACE

FRUIT   KINDNESS   SELF-CONTROL

GENTLENESS   LOVE   SPIRIT

```
        F S R       N K L
      K F R U I T H G N L B
      G T S S E N D O O G H N B
    F R F A I T H F U L N E S S M
  H L W K V M L H K P E A C E N L K
  Y O J M G E N T L E N E S S M W Q
  K V Q N R F G N P A T I E N C E M
  S E L F C O N T R O L K N D J S N
  G H D K T N D N V T T J K O G
    T K I N D N E S S D V N Y
    H G B N L J E E R F Q
      N S P I R I T W S
```

Find the answers on page 155

CROSSWORD PUZZLE

ACROSS

1. You can shine for Jesus by doing _____ things (Matthew 5:16)
3. God's Spirit gives us ____ and love and self-control (2 Timothy 1:7)
4. Paul told Timothy that even though he was young, he could be an example because of his _____ (1 Timothy 4:12)
5. The last good thing listed in the fruit of the Spirit (Galatians 5:23)
7. Jesus said that a branch needs to be connected to the _____ to bear fruit (John 15:4)
9. Kind words are sweet like _____ (Proverbs 16:24)

DOWN

1. What kind of answer turns away anger? (Proverbs 15:1)
2. Paul said some people were trying to be right with God by living according to the _____ instead of the Spirit (Galatians 5:4)
3. What should control our hearts and minds? (Colossians 3:15)
5. We receive fruit from the _____ (Galatians 5:22)
6. The first good thing listed in the fruit of the Spirit (Galatians 5:22)
8. What does God fill us with when we follow His ways? (Psalm 16:11)

Find the answers on page 156

Quiz 19
THE CHURCH

After Jesus went to heaven, His followers began to meet in homes to share meals, to pray together, and to talk about Jesus. This was the beginning of "going to church."

HOW MANY QUESTIONS CAN YOU ANSWER ABOUT THE START OF THE CHURCH?

1. **What did the first Christians pray for as they spread the good news about Jesus? (Acts 4:29)**
    a) for things to go smoothly
    b) for the king to like them
    c) for boldness to speak without fear
    d) for the ability to perform miracles

2. **Who was trying to destroy the new church by putting Christians in prison? (Acts 8:3)**
   a) Simon Peter
   b) Barnabas
   c) Barabbas
   d) Saul

3. **Where were Jesus's followers first called "Christians"? (Acts 11:26)**
   a) Antioch
   b) Athens
   c) Jerusalem
   d) Ephesus

4. **When did Saul, later called Paul, become a Christian? (Acts 9:3–5)**
   a) after hearing Peter preach a sermon
   b) after he saw Jesus's empty tomb
   c) after seeing a bright light and hearing Jesus speak
   d) after he was swallowed by a whale

5. **Who were the first missionaries sent out by the church? (Acts 13:2–3)**
   a) James and John
   b) Barnabas and Saul
   c) Barabbas and Paul
   d) David and Goliath

6. **How far did Jesus tell His disciples to spread the good news? (Acts 1:8)**
   a) throughout Asia
   b) as far as Egypt
   c) around Galilee
   d) to the ends of the earth

7. **What is another name for the church? (Colossians 1:18)**
   a) a group of angels
   b) the sword of the Spirit
   c) the body of Christ
   d) the big white building with a steeple

8. **What does the Bible say the church is built from? (Ephesians 2:19–22)**
   a) bricks and mortar
   b) stone and marble
   c) prayers and songs
   d) all of God's people

Find the answers on page 156

CROSSWORD PUZZLE

ACROSS

1. Where did some of the apostles end up because the high priest was jealous? (Acts 5:17–18)
3. Jesus is the corner_____ of the church—which means He is its most important part (1 Peter 2:7)
6. The church is the pillar and _____ of truth (1 Timothy 3:15)
7. Besides apostles and prophets, who did God give to the church? (1 Corinthians 12:28)
9. How often did the early church members meet in the temple courtyard? (Acts 2:46)
10. What did the first Christians do with the things they owned? (Acts 4:32)
11. The disciples never stopped teaching about Jesus in the _____ and from house to house (Acts 5:42)

DOWN

1. Who spoke to Saul on the road to Damascus? (Acts 9:4–5)
2. The apostles taught people about Jesus by speaking and writing _____ (2 Thessalonians 2:15)
4. The first Christians preached that Jesus is _____ (2 Corinthians 4:5)
5. As people believed in Jesus, they were _____ right away (Acts 18:8)
8. The first Christians ate and _____ together (Acts 2:42)

Find the answers on page 156

Help the disciples spread the gospel to the whole world!

Find the answer on page 157

WORD SEARCH
Can you find all the words?
Words may be forward, backward, or up-and-down.

ANTIOCH   CHRISTIANS   MISSIONARY

BAPTIZE   CHURCH   PREACH

BODY OF CHRIST   CORNERSTONE   SHARE

BOLDNESS   LETTERS   TEACHER

```
                H G
                R D T K
                H S H A R E
                R L E T T E R S
                T Q N H C A E R P K
T H N G X R T C H R I S T I A N S K Q B
E N S S E N D L O B H Z N H N K M N V A
A R H D T C H C O R N E R S T O N E Q P
C B M I S S I O N A R Y N H I G R S N T
H T N R S H C R U H C W K T O S Q N C I
E Q T R H S D M Q D F R H M C H C V B Z
R H B O D Y O F C H R I S T H K H K T E
```

Find the answers on page 157

Quiz 20
JESUS IS COMING BACK!

The Bible tells us that Jesus lived on earth a little more than thirty years before going back to heaven. But Jesus had told His followers that He would come back to earth someday. We don't know when Jesus is coming back, but we do know that He will.

TRY TO ANSWER THE FOLLOWING QUESTIONS ABOUT JESUS COMING BACK.
The Bible verses will help you.

1. **As Jesus was going to heaven, who told the disciples that Jesus would come back? (Acts 1:10–11)**
   a) Jesus's mother Mary
   b) the apostle Paul
   c) two men dressed in white
   d) Jewish leaders

2. **Who knows exactly when Jesus is going to return to earth? (Mark 13:32)**
   a) Christians
   b) Bible teachers
   c) the angels
   d) only God the Father

3. **Who is preparing a place for us in heaven? (John 14:1–2)**
   a) Abraham
   b) Simon Peter
   c) our great-great grandparents
   d) Jesus

4. **What should we do while we wait for Jesus to return? (Galatians 6:9–10)**
   a) play video games
   b) do good things for others
   c) listen to music
   d) watch TV

5. **Who will see Jesus when He returns? (Revelation 1:7)**
   a) missionaries
   b) pastors
   c) everyone who's awake at the time
   d) everyone

6. **What must happen before Jesus returns? (Matthew 24:14)**
   a) everyone needs to be baptized
   b) everyone will become a missionary
   c) everyone should read the Bible
   d) the good news of God's kingdom must be preached to all nations

7. **What will happen to God's children when Jesus returns? (1 John 3:2)**
   a) they will become like Jesus
   b) they will become like angels
   c) they will be afraid
   d) they will stay on earth

8. **What did Jesus say about His return? (Revelation 22:20)**
   a) He is coming soon
   b) He is coming in power
   c) He is going to fix up the mess
   d) He will swoop down like an eagle

Find the answers on page 158

FINISH THE PICTURE

Complete the scene by drawing angels rejoicing in heaven like John saw in the book of Revelation.

CROSSWORD PUZZLE

ACROSS

1. From what direction did the prophet Ezekiel say Jesus will return? (Ezekiel 43:1–2)
3. When Jesus comes back, Christians will be taken up into the _____ (1 Thessalonians 4:17)
5. Jesus will use His _____ to change our bodies to be like His (Philippians 3:21)
7. When Jesus comes from heaven it will be like _____ flashing in the sky (Matthew 24:27)
8. When Jesus returns for His people, He will wipe away every _____ from their eyes (Revelation 21:4)
11. How long will we be with Jesus after he returns? (1 Thessalonians 4:17)
12. Jesus said He will make everything _____ (Revelation 21:5)

DOWN

2. What instrument will sound when Jesus returns? (Matthew 24:31)
4. Who will be coming with Jesus when He returns? (Matthew 16:27)
6. What color were the clothes of the men who told the disciples Jesus would come back? (Acts 1:10–11)
9. When Jesus returns, He will _____ us for the good things we have done (Revelation 22:12)
10. Where is our true homeland? (Philippians 3:20)

Find the answers on page 158

WORD SEARCH
Can you find all the words?
Words may be forward, backward, or up-and-down.

EAST	HEAVEN	REVELATION
EVERYONE	JESUS	RULE
EZEKIEL	PREPARE	SOMEDAY
FATHER	RETURN	WAIT

```
H N D W R T J E S U S T K S Z E Q N B W
Y A D E M O S L H T J C B R F A H R S A
K B V D R E T U R N H R T J R S K L M I
F A T H E R X N P H N E Z N J T D R B T
N B H D K N E V A E H L G Z F N J U N R
D M E V E R Y O N E N T B S Y P L L N T
M L E I K E Z E M W B P L Z F H N E V R
N D G H P R E P A R E K N W L T H N C T
N B H R D G C B K L R E V E L A T I O N
```

Find the answers on page 158

QUIZZES & GAMES
ANSWER KEY

QUIZ 1

1. c   2. a   3. b   4. b   5. b   6. d   7. c   8. d

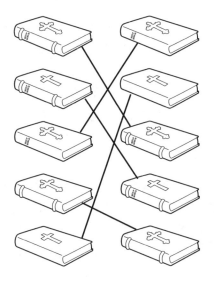

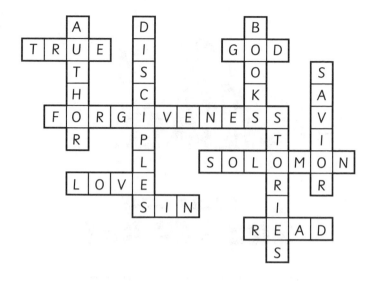

Crossword puzzle:

```
          A         D              B
   T R U E          I          G O D            S
          T         S          O                A
          H         C          K                V
   F O R G I V E N E S S                        I
          R         P          T                I
                    L      S O L O M O N
       L O V E              O              R
                    S I N   R
                            I
                        R E A D
                            S
```

Word search grid:

W Y M T C R D I S C I P L E S M W V H Q
X M W M P D R T I K P T N L U K E C Y P
Y Q M D O M T X I R L T I M O R F Q R J
B C W M P S X B T V T L I N V C R W S E
I W X Q Z B E L P C V V T S B R Y P M S
B F K B W Q D S Q D S Z R U Q O L L I U
L K X M B D B P P K C G V G O D L T T S
E F R H D M N T T J B B D M L O Q X L R
L K T M B A U T H O R K L N M P B D R H
K T B Q N J W M H R B S N B Q M B X S F
W T E S T A M E N T W L T N P X K H C P
M P R O P H E T S M M N X T L T P N D A
Q T K N W S T Q P S A L M S D C H F Q U
K X V F M G D B K L R T S M B O O K S L

QUIZ 2

1. a   2. c   3. d   4. b   5. d   6. a   7. c   8. b

```
Y  O  U  G  R  S  M  H  H  E
A  V  I  E  P  N  O  L  S  Y
T  R  K  I  N  D  T  F  I  A
L  H  R  T  D  S  H  C  F  H
E  I  A  U  R  U  E  H  A  L
T  R  O  N  D  S  R  I  D  E
A  L  D  R  K  E  Y  L  O  L
C  K  I  N  O  J  W  D  O  S
A  B  E  R  A  C  L  R  G  L
Y  O  U  R  N  E  D  E  D  S
```

Secret Message: Your heavenly Father already knows all your needs.

```
      G  H  N                  S  O  N
      B  E  V  O  L            L  M  G  S  Q
      D  V  B  Y  H  R  S      M  F  A  M  I  L  Y
      V  D  B  S  U  N  S  E  T     Y  P  L  K  J  H  N  O  E
      S  C  D  X  Z  D  F  R  T  H  A  M  A  Z  I  N  G  B  D  S
C  R  E  A  T  O  R  K  P  K  L  M  F  B  Y  S  Q  C  B  N  L  V
B  B  O  D  Y  O  F  C  H  R  I  S  T  N  H  N  B  M  T  H  H  B
X  D  S  Z  W  R  T  H  Y  M  A  S  T  E  R  P  I  E  C  E  X  N
D  N  C  H  I  L  D  R  E  N  O  F  G  O  D  N  H  B  P  D  M  N
      N  H  B  P  D  C  E  L  H  N  M  B  F  A  H  T  R  V  C  N
      R  F  S  D  W  P  L  K  J  H  G  D  S  N  K  Q  D  B
      D  R  T  W  O  N  D  E  R  F  U  L  H  P  L  K
      H  Y  H  G  B  N  R  W  D  B  N  M  T  H
      H  G  B  R  E  H  T  A  F  M  D  S
      N  D  R  F  E  E  H  T  B  V
      B  W  O  R  L  D  T  H
      C  B  N  R  T  D
      R  D  W  S
      C  D
```

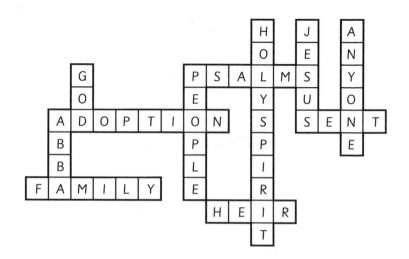

QUIZ 3

1. c   2. b   3. c   4. d   5. b   6. a   7. d   8. c

E C P K L S R B P N
S Q P E O P L E M N X Z
G O O D P M S S T A R S D L
R T Q C T M Q B C S N S M T T H
Y T W F T G A R D E N P X M R R T M
T P L C X A N I M A L S X W E Q V T
K N L G T D M O O N T R L T E X Z R
W A T E R Q H G N M P L K W S F X C
T C X L M P L A N T S T B B W T R Y
R T L I G H T S D C T I I Z X S
T N Q V X Z S Q D T R R K D
F G B H H U T Y L P D C
O B N H N Z H B D S

QUIZ 4

1. c 2. a 3. b 4. d 5. b 6. c 7. a 8. d

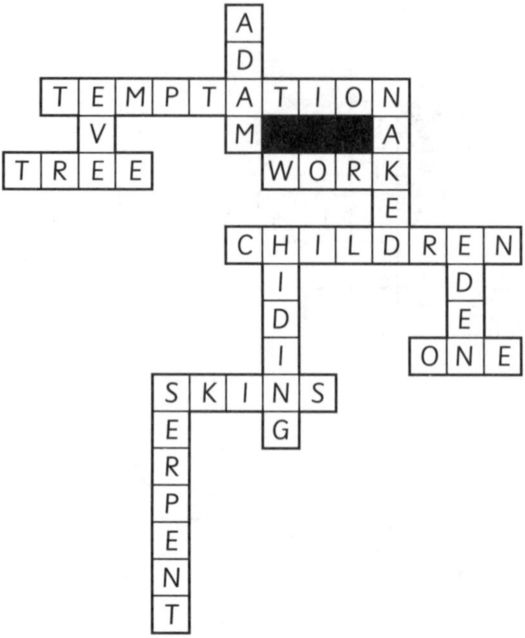

ADAM
TEMPTATION
EVE
TREE
NAKED
WORK
CHILDREN
HIDING
EDEN
ONE
SKINS
SERPENT

G	A	D	M	A	S	D	F	K	L	P	O	C	L	O	T	H	E	S
A	N	O	I	H	W	A	B	N	I	W	E	B	T	S	E	M	O	I
R	F	S	S	E	N	E	V	I	G	R	O	F	L	A	B	S	T	K
D	A	N	L	N	S	W	E	L	T	L	Y	J	E	T	D	H	O	T
E	L	A	E	H	L	T	I	N	S	E	L	E	O	W	I	A	H	U
N	M	K	Y	I	D	R	Y	E	A	L	O	D	M	H	S	U	M	H
L	T	E	M	P	T	A	T	I	O	N	M	A	S	T	O	E	D	S
E	M	N	I	E	K	M	R	L	V	G	C	U	N	M	B	T	H	A
S	O	W	L	H	I	D	E	U	F	I	T	N	E	V	E	D	E	R
I	T	H	M	U	A	S	E	B	R	C	K	A	W	I	Y	B	A	O
A	O	S	N	C	E	I	H	A	F	R	U	I	T	V	E	H	O	N

QUIZ 5

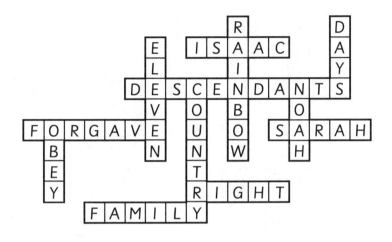

```
H G T L S L A V E D V B C W A X S B M Q F
L D G B V C X Z W N A T I O N M B W Q G L
C H R R E B N M K P C Q W R T Y P M K G O
N B U V D N A T P C N M H B K L P K W B O
O X L D W Q S T M T P Y G E D W S Z Q R D
A F E T H W M Q B A R K T H G D S W Q S T
H G R B B Q V W N R Q G H G E N E S I S M
Y R T H G D C B M J O S E P H W G H M Q L
S G H K L A B R A H A M M R H P N I A R B
S P R B R H P R O M I S E Q T B T H L N T
```

QUIZ 6

1. d   2. d   3. a   4. a   5. d   6. c   7. d   8. c

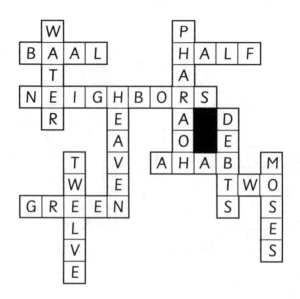

QUIZ 7

1. c   2. a   3. c   4. b   5. c   6. d   7. a   8. d

JOSHUA

ESTHER

DANIEL

NOAH

MOSES

ELIJAH

WIDOW

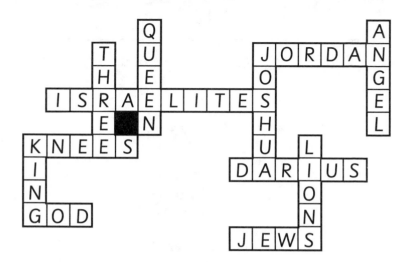

QUIZ 8

1. d   2. c   3. c   4. b   5. d   6. a   7. c   8. b

For the **LORD** grants **WISDOM**! From His **MOUTH** come **KNOWLEDGE** and **UNDERSTANDING**

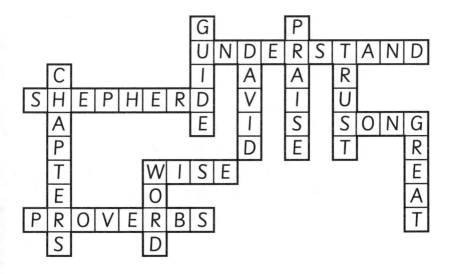

QUIZ 9

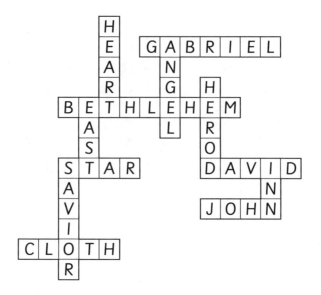

1. c   2. a   3. b   4. c   5. d   6. a   7. c   8. d

Start   End

```
G B N M K L P Y T R W S Q S H I N E M B
B D W T H G I L D O M G Q E H N T C L Y
T M U S T A R D L C R M N E B G P C E K
W R E J O I C E M K Q W G D D H G N X Z
P N C G R E L B M U H M T S B W Q B S X
S A M A R I T A N S H W X F G R E W O S
R T B D H E A V E N N R G K I N G D O M
B G R T B M C H R I S T I A N M K L P B
```

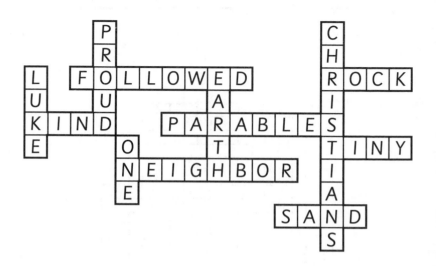

QUIZ 11

1. a   2. c   3. d   4. b   5. d   6. c   7. b   8. a

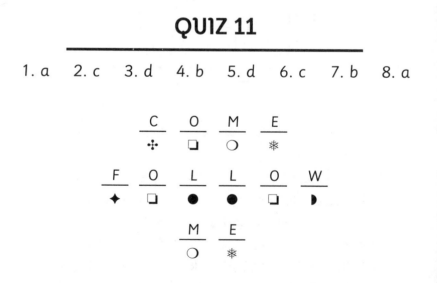

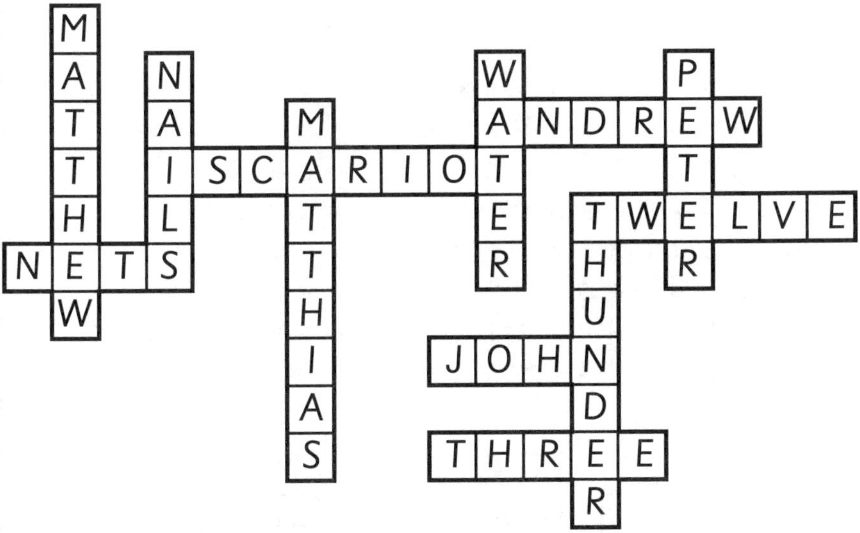
MATTHEW
NAILS
ISCARIOT
MATTHIAS
WATER
ANDREW
PETER
TWELVE
NETS
THUNDER
JOHN
THREE

Q	N	R	G	P	E	T	E	R	K	N	D	B	W	R	S	T	P	D	W
H	B	D	G	P	T	A	X	C	O	L	L	E	C	T	O	R	M	N	B
A	D	B	W	T	W	E	L	V	E	H	K	D	N	H	O	J	B	E	M
N	M	D	D	I	S	C	I	P	L	E	M	W	N	D	S	Q	N	T	S
D	B	R	B	R	O	T	H	E	R	S	H	A	M	Q	P	K	L	S	H
S	W	L	L	Q	W	O	L	L	O	F	H	T	W	P	Q	H	R	S	G
F	M	F	G	Q	V	Z	X	F	I	S	H	E	R	M	E	N	N	F	H
R	E	D	N	U	H	T	M	N	P	L	K	R	M	H	R	P	T	E	P

1. c   2. d   3. b   4. c   5. a   6. d   7. d   8. b

D B M K L S A I L B O A T G R H N V J M
B R D S W R T P K H S I F M N A I N M A
N E K S Q N Q T S M P L T D G R K B C R
N A Z M I R A C L E M P R N S T Q B D Y
D D K L A Z A R U S N P L S M E D S B Q
P G H S T O R M N B L Y G P B N K L N O
D B N G H P T R T M A R T H A Q D J T Y
H B E H E A L E D M H E L P O E P R D J

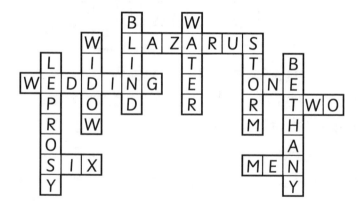

QUIZ 13

1. a   2. c   3. d   4. b   5. b   6. d   7. c   8. a

Our **FATHER** in heaven,
Hallowed be Your **NAME**.
Your **KINGDOM** come,
Your **WILL** be done
on **EARTH** as it is in **HEAVEN**.
Give us this day our daily **BREAD**.
And **FORGIVE** us our debts,
as we **FORGIVE** our debtors.
And do not lead us into temptation,
but deliver us from the **EVIL** one.
For Yours is the **KINGDOM** and the
POWER and the **GLORY** forever.
Amen.

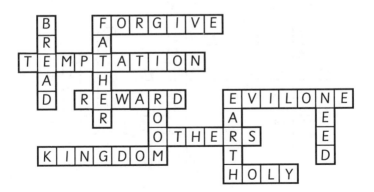

Q N E E D L W D T F G S R T
G H K M N B R E A D H Q K B D D
G B H Q W D S N M O D G N I K N A B
D F G W Q P R A Y E R B W M T L T I D B
N E V A E H H M R G R H D B K T X L T N
F M F O R G I V E W Q O M N K X T Y V T
D S R R O O D B C D W L N B G R W B X C
F A T H E R N B D Q Y Q E A R T H W
G T M V L R C K E E D N W S B M
N T E M P T A T I O N R S M

QUIZ 14

1. c   2. b   3. d   4. b   5. a   6. c   7. c   8. b

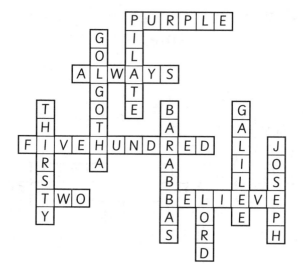

```
        U B L A R H P J
        Z E N O T S N M
        R L Y J A S H E
        N S I L V E R L
K E A R T H Q U A K E O T R Q K U H
P X G N S S O R C H M B T W I L M E
Y M C I H S O W N W L B E R Y K A J
L V P R I E S T S H U E L S N I T O
I T E O B A I F L E T R U T W S M C
Q S P A W O H G N Q R S F S H U T W
        B W O M E N J C
        C Z A N G E L I
        F D C R O W N T
        M H U B W O D S
        E Q G U A R D H
        X T O M B R L K
        H A N D W E G O
        V Y E P O K N W
        G D A R K L O M
        E J U S M R Q Y
```

QUIZ 15

1. b   2. c   3. a   4. d   5. b   6. c   7. d   8. c

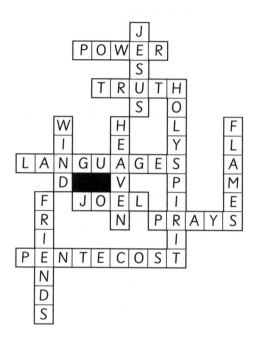

Crossword grid words: JESUS, POWER, TRUTH, HOLY, WIND, HEAVEN, LANGUAGES, FLAME, SPIRIT, JOEL, FRIENDS, PRAYS, PENTECOST

Word Search:

```
D H K M R H T U R T S N V J E S U S Q W
G W K L D S Z W C B P O W E R T L S Z M
Q M I K N D S E M A L F M W H P T N T Q
B D H N Q W F R I E N D S D W O P L N V
D X C B D M K S P I R I T H W L L B V S
W B Q D I S C I P L E S W N Q B H Y N L
R E P L E H M K H C H R I S T I A N N B
M N B L A N G U A G E M W P T L J S Z Q
```

QUIZ 16

1. a   2. c   3. c   4. d   5. b   6. a   7. b   8. d

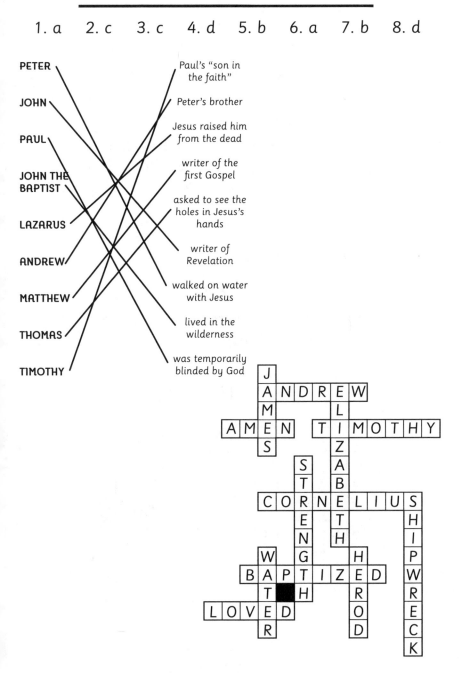

PETER — walked on water with Jesus
JOHN — writer of Revelation
PAUL — was temporarily blinded by God
JOHN THE BAPTIST — lived in the wilderness
LAZARUS — Jesus raised him from the dead
ANDREW — Peter's brother
MATTHEW — writer of the first Gospel
THOMAS — asked to see the holes in Jesus's hands
TIMOTHY — Paul's "son in the faith"

Paul's "son in the faith"

Peter's brother

Jesus raised him from the dead

writer of the first Gospel

asked to see the holes in Jesus's hands

writer of Revelation

walked on water with Jesus

lived in the wilderness

was temporarily blinded by God

Crossword answers:
JAMES (down)
ANDREW
AMEN
TIMOTHY
ELIZABETH (down)
STRENGTH (down)
CORNELIUS
SHIPWRECK (down)
WATER (down)
BAPTIZED
HEROD (down)
LOVED

S M N L O C U S T S B Q R T P K C D S R
A H W X D S B A P T I Z E G K P B M T O
U K B N O I T A L E V E R H G T N W T C
L B D F G P D A M A S C U S L N S X N K
H S H I P W R E C K M N S H P T N X S T
N O M I S B D G E E D E B E Z K H M R P
B H D P R E P A R E M B Q P I L L A R Q
H B Q N R P T P A T M O S T L N N T S D

QUIZ 17:

1. d   2. c   3. b   4. a   5. d   6. c   7. c   8. d

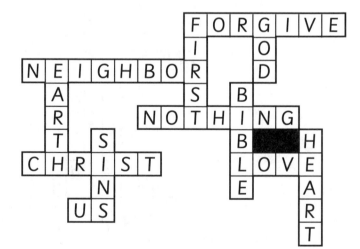

```
        I L O              K E L
      B E V J A          G O D S Q
    D V M I N D S        M C N T H L Y
  V D B T U H S A J    Y P H E A R T O E
  S C E V O L F R T H F M A O I R G U D S
K R E A T S R K P K C H I L D R E N B N L H
C Y M B A L F C W O B S A N H N B M T H H B
X D S R O B H G I E N S M E R H K W C E X N
O H C W I H D A E B O S G F O R E V E R M S
  N H C O M M A N D M E N T A H T R V C N
    R F S D W P L K J H G D S N K Q D B
      D R B E O I D S O U L T H P L O
      H Y H G B N T W D B N M T H
      H G B P A T I E N T D S
        B D R F A C H T B T
        W D N I K T H G
          C B N R T D
            R L W U
              C D
```

QUIZ 18

1. c   2. b   3. a   4. c   5. a   6. d   7. b   8. d

```
        F S R        N K L
      K F R U I T H G N L B
    G T S S E N D O O G H N B
  F R F A I T H F U L N E S S M
H L W K V M L H K P E A C E N L K
Y O J M G E N T L E N E S S M W Q
K V Q N R F G N P A T I E N C E M
S E L F C O N T R O L K N D J S N
  G H D K T N D N V T T J K O G
    T K I N D N E S S D V N Y
      H G B N L J E E R F Q
        N S P I R I T W S
```

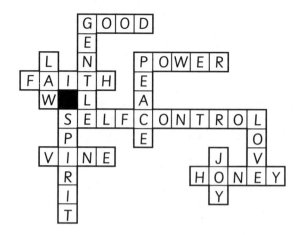

QUIZ 19

1. c   2. d   3. a   4. c   5. b   6. d   7. c   8. d

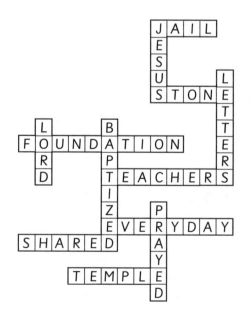

H G
R D T K
H SHARE
R LETTERS
T Q N H C A E R P K

T H N G X R T C H R I S T I A N S K Q B
E N S S E N D L O B H Z N H N K M N V A
A R H D T C H C O R N E R S T O N E Q P
C B M I S S I O N A R Y N H I G R S N T
H T N R S H C R U H C W K T O S Q N C I
E Q T R H S D M Q D F R H M C H C V B Z
R H B O D Y O F C H R I S T H K H K T E

QUIZ 20

1. c 2. d 3. d 4. b 5. d 6. d 7. a 8. a

```
E A S T
      R
C L O U D S
      M
  A   P O W E R
  N   E   ■ H
L I G H T N I N G
  E       I
  L     T E A R
  S       E
          W
      H   A
F O R E V E R   D
      A       
      V
    N E W
      N
```

```
H N D W R T J E S U S T K S Z E Q N B W
Y A D E M O S L H T J C B R F A H R S A
K B V D R E T U R N H R T J R S K L M I
F A T H E R X N P H N E Z N J T D R B T
N B H D K N E V A E H L G Z F N J U N R
D M E V E R Y O N E N T B S Y P L L N T
M L E I K E Z E M W B P L Z F H N E V R
N D G H P R E P A R E K N W L T H N C T
N B H R D G C B K L R E V E L A T I O N
```

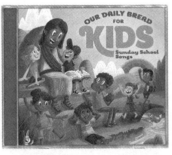

COLORING & ACTIVITY BOOK **MATCHING GAME**

Visit dhp.org/odbkids to order!

Discovery House.
from Our Daily Bread Ministries